LESSONS
from the
LEGENDS of
WALL STREET

HOW WARREN BUFFETT,
BENJAMIN GRAHAM, PHIL FISHER,
T. ROWE PRICE, AND JOHN TEMPLETON
CAN HELP YOU GROW RICH

NIKKI ROSS, CFP

MJF BOOKS
NEW YORK

Published by MJF Books
Fine Communications
322 Eighth Avenue
New York, NY 10001

Lessons From the Legends of Wall Street
LC Control Number 2002104332
ISBN 1-56731-540-2

This edition published by arrangement with Dearborn, a Kaplan
Professional Company

Manufactured in the United States of America on acid-free paper ∞

MJF Books and the MJF colophon are trademarks of Fine Creative Media, Inc.

BG   10 9   8   7   6   5   4   3   2   1

Advance Praise for
Lessons from the Legends of Wall Street

"Provides unprecedented insights into the best financial minds
of our time . . . must reading for all investors."

Christopher L. Hayes, Ph.D.
Founder and Director, National Center for Women & Retirement Research

"All investors can benefit from studying how others have made
fortunes in the market, and *Lessons from the Legends* is an
excellent way to discover the strategies of five of America's best known
stock market investors. Use this book to see how you can adapt the
strategies of Graham, Buffett, Price, and the others to help your own
portfolios. You will surely benefit from it."

Stephen Sanborn
Director of Research, Value Line Publishing, Inc.

"Over a 35 year career in equity investing, I have come across
few books which I have found to be useful. This book is one
of the few. It belongs on my very short list of recommended
reading for any serious investor."

Philip K. Swigard
Berkshire Hathaway Shareholder and Private Investor

"If you want to understand literature, you study the great authors;
music, the great composers. Why, then, do most investment courses
ignore the great investors and instead preach the efficient market
theory, which tells us no one can beat the market and ignore those
who do? Thankfully, Nikki Ross's *Lessons from the Legends of Wall
Street* helps to right the score. You'll find more practical advice in
this one book than in a dozen academic investment texts."

Don Phillips
CEO, Morningstar, Inc.

"Well done! An excellent book for the investing public. The blend of
biography and academic text is unique. It makes learning more fun."

T. Wayne Whipple, CFA
Executive Director, The New York Society of Security Analysts, Inc.

"Articulating lessons from the deans of the investment world, this wonderful how-to book is a remarkable resource for investors."

Bernadette B. Murphy
Chief Market Analyst, Kimelman & Baird LLC and
Regular panelist on *Wall $treet Week With Louis Rukeyser*

"The markets always remind us of the necessity of wise investment counsel. The insights offered by the investment Dream Team put together by Nikki Ross are as timely as they are brilliant. The wisdom and insights of these five legends can help consultants, money managers, financial advisors, stockbrokers, and most importantly the investor, develop successful investment strategies. I thoroughly enjoyed reading this outstanding and informative book and recommend it to all types of investors."

Michael T. Dieschbourg
CIMA, Consulting Group, Salomon Smith Barney

"Nikki Ross has meticulously mined the gold from some of the richest veins in modern times—and has refined it in a way that makes it valuable for all who want to invest intelligently. She's made required reading for the experienced investor understandable for the novice."

Ellis Traub
Chairman, Inve$tWare Corporation

"Entertaining and informative, five legendary investors speak to you through Nikki Ross. She details the strategies they used to acquire and preserve their fortunes and explains how you can create your own blueprint for wealth. I highly recommend it."

Gail Liberman
Syndicated columnist and author of *Rags to Riches: Motivating Stories of How Ordinary People Achieved Extraordinary Wealth!*

DEDICATION

To God, the giver of all wisdom

To my husband, Joseph, for his love

To my mother, Claire, for her courage

To my brother, Richard, for his devotion

CONTENTS

PREFACE

SPEAKING AT AN investment management conference in Miami, Florida, John Templeton, predicted, "The Dow Jones Industrial Average will be over 1,000,000 by the end of the 21st century." I noticed the raised eyebrows, wide-eyed expressions, and quizzical looks of some in the audience, yet from a historical perspective his rationale is realistic. At the beginning of the 20th century, the Dow was approximately 100 in round numbers and on the day he spoke, November 18, 1999, the Index was 10,600, an increase of over 100 times. If the Dow increases by the same amount in this century as the last, it will reach 1,000,000 by the year 2099.

Although Templeton was optimistic about the future of the stock market, he warned, "Be prepared [emotionally and financially] for 21st century bear markets." Generally, bear markets are defined as market declines of 20 percent or more and can be caused by various factors, such as higher inflation and interest rates, lower corporate earnings, and a negative change in investor psychology (for details of Templeton's speech, see Chapter 29). Templeton's warning was timely, because signs of a bear market appeared in the spring of 2000.

Even if you invest when the market is going up, you may not be in the right stocks. According to Anthony Dwyer, a market strategist with a Wall Street brokerage firm, the Dow rose 25 percent in 1999, but 60 percent of the stocks on the New York Stock Exchange did not increase.[1]

How This Book Can Help You

The wisdom of five legendary investors is condensed into three vital steps for investing, along with advice on how you can apply their strategies in any market climate—up, down, or sideways. You will find information to help you make better investment decisions, whether you are a novice or a sophisticated investor, buying individual stocks, mutual funds, or employing a money manager.

You may be familiar with one or more of the legends featured; however, this book contains updated, modern applications of their strategies. Chapters about them provide different, essential investing knowledge and principles that can be combined to create a sound investment plan:

- Warren Buffett, a self-made billionaire who created an extraordinary long-term investment track record, gives insights about how to profit from reading annual reports and what to look for in stock research reports.
- Benjamin Graham, the father of value investing who became rich by developing and applying criteria for security analysis, explains the important financial numbers and ratios necessary to evaluate a company. Graham's followers give expanded criteria for 21st-century investing.
- Phil Fisher, who made his fortune with a detective-like investment method, tells how to pick stocks with tremendous profit potential by evaluating a company's top executives, products, and policies.
- Thomas Rowe Price, a futurist who acquired his fortune investing in growth stocks and applying the life-cycle theory of companies (birth, maturity, decline), discusses the warning signals of slowing growth and the trends affecting stocks. Money managers at T. Rowe Price Associates, the mutual fund group Price founded, update and expand his advice.
- John Templeton, the dean of global investing and founder of the Templeton Funds and the Templeton Foundation, who

has created spiritual as well as material wealth, shares 15 timeless investment rules and strategies for global investing.

How This Book Is Organized

Parts I through V begin with an overview of each man and his accomplishments. Next, you will find a description of their success strategies and investment principles, followed by a discussion of how they apply the 3 Steps:

1. *Gather the Information,* details how the legends find leads and research companies and how you can research stocks using the Internet, print publications, and other sources of information.

2. *Evaluate the Information,* describes how they apply their criteria. You will learn how these great investors look at quantitative information—the financial numbers of a business—and how they assess qualitative information—the quality of a firm's management and products. Descriptions of companies they have bought are used as examples (they may not own these stocks by the time you are reading this book and the company's fundamentals and stock price may not justify purchase). You will also discover that the legends have similar criteria for financial numbers such as sales and earnings, profit margins, and return on shareholders' equity; however, there are differences in the way they look at financial information.

3. *Make the Decision,* discusses how they make buy, hold, and sell decisions.

Additional chapters include material unique to each man, descriptions of how to apply the strategies based on your own investment profile—conservative, moderate, or aggressive (for help in deciding your category, see the Investor Profile Questionnaire, at the end of Chapter 32)—and a brief narrative about their lives and careers. You can begin by reading the overview and information concerning the investment strategies or go directly to the 3 Steps. If you want to know more about the backgrounds of the legends, you can read the biographical information first.

In Part VI you will find out how to apply a composite version of the 3 Steps and gain information to create your own blueprint for wealth.

Author's Acknowledgments: Research, Interviews, and Contributions

I would like to thank the following people for their contributions:

Warren Buffett and Debbie Bosanek, his assistant, invited me to Berkshire Hathaway's annual meetings and provided past annual reports and other material for the chapters about Buffett.

David Catalan, executive director of the Omaha Press Club, and Gary Harper, working with the Press Club, invited me to speak at the club, along with two other authors, Andrew Kilpatrick and Janet Lowe, recapping Buffett's and Munger's speeches after the 1998 annual meeting of Berkshire Hathaway. Preparing for the speech gave me greater insight into how Buffett and Munger invest.

John Spears and Robert Q. Wyckoff, Jr., of Tweedy Browne and Mason Hawkins and Lee Harper at Southeastern Asset Management furnished material and advice for the chapters about Benjamin Graham. John Bajkowski, editor of *Computerized Investing,* who has written about Graham, contributed an article about financial ratio analysis that he wrote for the *AAII Journal* (American Association of Individual Investors).

Special thanks to Phil Fisher (Fisher asked that I refer to him as Phil instead of Philip). He is one of the most conscientious people I know and spent hours of his time on the phone, through faxes, and by letters, answering my questions. I would also like to thank Phil's son, Ken, CEO of Fisher Investments and a popular columnist for *Forbes* magazine, as well as Sherri, Ken's wife, and Clay, their son, for their help.

George Roche, chairman of T. Rowe Price Associates; his assistant, Joan Flister; David Testa chief investment officer; Bob Smith, who manages Price's original fund; and Steve Norwitz, vice president; assisted with chapters about the company's founder, Thomas Rowe Price. Norwitz gave me permission to use some of Price's writings, data from an unpublished history of T. Rowe Price Associates, and publications of the company.

John Templeton was so kind as to contribute some of his writings. I am grateful for our phone conversations and the time I spent with Templeton at the Institutional Investment Management Summit, November 1999, which helped me to learn more about him. Don Reed, president of Templeton Investment Council; Mark Holowesko, director of global equity research and money manager for some of the Franklin Templeton funds; Charles Johnson, CEO of Franklin Resources; and John Galbraith, former chairman of Templeton Management Company, provided information and comments for the chapters about Templeton. Mary Walker, Templeton's assistant, has been very gracious.

Thomas E. O'Hara chairman of the National Association of Investors Corporation and his wife, Eleanor, gave me encouragement. And thanks to Cindy Zigmund, Jack Kiburz, and Trey Thoelcke at Dearborn, who worked on this project. Additional acknowledgments continue after the last chapter.

I hope you enjoy reading this book as much as I enjoyed writing it and you find great benefit from the lessons of these legendary investors.

PART I

Warren Buffett: The Super Combination Investor

One of America's richest men, Warren Buffett has had an incredible long-term track record of investment success since he began investing in 1956. Referred to as the Superman of Investors, Buffett reads and interprets corporate reports at high speeds, has an uncanny memory for numbers, and makes crucial investment decisions during jittery, jarring markets, with nerves of steel; his personality is also like Clark Kent's—mild mannered.

The epitome of the American dream, Buffett's rise from humble beginnings to great wealth hasn't changed his modest lifestyle, good old-fashioned morals, homespun humor, and down-to-earth wisdom. Making money was more of a necessity for Buffett in his early years, but later became much like a game with money as the scorecard. Although Buffett enjoys the good things in life, he doesn't overindulge. He still lives in the same house he bought for about $32,000. Buffett's idea of the use of money is that if you spend a dollar today, you are also spending the compounded value of that dollar many years from today. He has selected stocks wisely and applied the principle of compound interest to investing.

Buffett didn't establish his track record of investment success alone. He studied the strategies of other great investors and combined them with his own expertise. Investors with less-than-super investment powers can emulate his techniques and also create outstanding investment profits.

Realistically defining his level of competency, Buffett only invests in businesses he understands; only those that make economic sense to him. When Buffett can't find investments meeting his criteria, he sits on the sidelines in a cash position looking for buying opportunities.

In 1956, he started his career managing an investment partnership. Thirteen years later, he sold most of his stocks. His partnership had increased at an annual compounded rate of about 23.8 percent compared with 9 percent for the Dow Jones Industrial Average, and Buffett's net worth amounted to $25 million. During this time, speculation was rampant, stocks were dangerously high, and he wanted to protect profits for himself and his partners.

Between 1973 and 1974, when the Dow Jones Industrial Average sank over 40 percent, Buffett had the money to make incredible buys. As chairman of Berkshire Hathaway, a corporation Buffett controlled and turned into a holding company, he purchased stocks of public companies and private firms. In 1973, Buffett invested about $10 million in shares of The Washington Post after the stock had dropped approximately 30 percent. He also acquired the Buffalo News. After the stock of GEICO Corporation crashed from $60 to $2 a share in 1976, Buffett began buying. GEICO made a great recovery, and about two decades later he bought the remaining shares, thereby acquiring the whole company. Buffett also purchased shares of Capital Cities/ ABC (Capital Cities was later acquired by Disney), Gillette, American Express, Freddie Mac, Coca-Cola, and others.

Although Buffett buys stocks, he sometimes invests in bonds, and in 1996, he invested in silver at about $4.25 an ounce. In 1998, he acquired International Dairy Queen. He also acquired General Re, a world leader in the property/casualty reinsurance business. With Berkshire Hathaway stock as currency, this transaction involved the equivalent of $22 billion.

Now a multibillionaire, Buffett also has created real wealth for those who invested with him and held for the long term. According to a *Forbes* article, October 11, 1999, $10,000 invested in Berkshire Hathaway in 1965 had grown to $51 million.[1]

Purchase companys traded need appeal to human Emotions Highly favorable image

Buffett's Success Strategies: Building Real Wealth with Commonsense Investment Rules and Compound Returns

BUFFETT THINKS OF buying stocks as if he were buying a piece of business to hold for the long term. He looks for companies that have a track record of financial success, quality management, a wide competitive advantage, and superior brand-name products used repeatedly. Generally, he purchases firms generating dependable streams of earnings that can be reinvested to grow the business and produce high returns on money invested by shareholders. Before buying a stock, Buffett asks: "Is this a wonderful business? Is the stock selling at a reasonable price?"

Buy Companies with User-Friendly Products That Capture Mind Share and Market Share

Marketing professor Robert Peterson researched customer satisfaction for years but found no evidence to prove it leads to repeat business. Then, Peterson discovered that a connection between customer satisfaction and repeat business occurs when an emotional link develops between the customer and the product or service.[1]

Buffett buys companies with products that fill the basic needs of society, appeal to human emotions, and evoke highly favorable images.

Gillette fills a basic need, for instance, and is associated with grooming. For many people, craving chocolate equates to eating a See's candy and being thirsty creates a mental image of a Coca-Cola drink. Firms such as these have established brand-name images through the years with their powerful advertising and intelligent marketing. Their products are in the public consciousness, which helps create a barrier to competition.

Generally, Buffett is a customer of the companies he purchases. Before he acquired the Nebraska Furniture Mart, Buffett shopped there for many years. At Berkshire Hathaway's annual meetings, nibbling a See's candy, holding a Coca-Cola in one hand and a Dairy Queen soft ice cream cone in the other, Buffett jokes about putting his money where his mouth is.

High-perceived value of products tends to give companies the ability to pass on higher costs to customers during inflationary times, and to sell products during recessions when customers might otherwise cut back on purchases.

Buy Companies with Quality Management

Buying a company with inept management can be like buying a train with no tracks to run on. Intelligent executives focus on their core business strengths instead of being involved with businesses outside their level of competency. Managers of firms Buffett has bought are focused, love what they do, and treat shareholders, customers, and employees fairly. Rose Blumkin, founder of Nebraska Furniture Mart, has a fitting motto, "Sell cheap and tell the truth." In addition, executives who work for the firm go out of their way to find products that fill customer needs. Employees are specially trained to provide quality customer service.

Buffett's Investment Rationale and Strategies

Although Buffett has refined and modified his strategies over the years, he continues to make purchases when he perceives value, whether in stocks or bonds, private or public companies, or other holdings. Some Buffett followers watch what he buys and follow his lead. But it is important to understand the investment criteria and strategies he has applied as well as the significance of his purchases. Buffett's purchase of silver, for instance, was widely publicized in the press. During Berkshire Hathaway's 1998 annual meeting, vice chairman Charlie Munger pointed out that the purchase only represented about 2 percent of Berkshire's assets and the impact on total asset value at the time was minimal. Besides, media speculation about Buffett's investment moves is not always correct.

Berkshire Hathaway's 1998 annual report listed common stock holdings with a value of over $750 million. The reported stock positions were American Express, Coca-Cola, Disney (was sold in 1999), Freddie Mac, Gillette, The Washington Post, and Wells Fargo.

Among privately held firms were GEICO and General Re in the insurance category and Flight Safety and Executive Jet in the flight services group. Nebraska Furniture Mart, R.C. Willey Home Furnishings, and Star Furniture Company were listed in the home furnishings category. The shoe group included H.H. Brown Shoe Company, Lowell Shoe, and Dexter Shoe Company, while the jewelry group included Helzberg's Diamond Shops and Borsheim's. Other private holdings were International Dairy Queen, See's Candies, Scott Fetzer Companies (World Book encyclopedias, Campbell Hausfeld air compressors, Kirby home cleaning systems), and the Buffalo News.

Being an independent thinker, Buffett has purchased stocks when many investors didn't recognize the value or were even negative about the companies. Two strategies he has applied, buying exceptional turnaround candidates and purchasing companies during bear markets that he believed had great long-term potential, are illustrated next.

Buy Exceptional Turnaround Candidates

Buffett bought shares of Wells Fargo in 1990. Known as the oldest bank in the west, Wells Fargo is a holding company based in California with operations in banking, mortgages, trust services, credit cards, and securities brokerage.

Fans of western movies and history buffs may recall tales of masked bandits who robbed stagecoaches carrying valuable cargo in Wells Fargo security boxes. The company traces its history back to 1852. After gold was discovered in 1848 at John Sutter's sawmill near Coloma, California, people from all over the country traveled to the area, lured by the prospect of profits. Among them were two successful eastern businessmen, Henry Wells and William G. Fargo, who watched the crowds prospecting for gold and devised another way to make their fortunes. On March 18, 1852, they started Wells Fargo & Co., a banking and express firm.

Wells Fargo survived the financial panic of 1855 when there was a run on several California banks, as well as the great California earthquake of 1906.[2] When Buffett bought its stock, Wells Fargo was going through another type of crisis. In 1990, California was in a recession and real estate values were very depressed. Wells Fargo had a large percentage of its loans in real estate. Investors questioned the value of these loans and some were even concerned about the bank's future solvency. Wells Fargo's stock dropped over 30 percent and Buffett bought. He thought that CEO Carl Reichard and his management team could guide the firm through the crisis. Under the leadership of Reichard, the bank instituted a cost-cutting program, reducing the number of employees as well as changing the compensation structure, and created other sources of revenue with additional banking services. Buffett purchased this stock below book value (net worth) per share. California pulled out of the recession and the real estate market recovered. Having added to his original purchase, Buffett invested $392 million in Wells Fargo. This investment was worth $2.39 billion at the end of 1999. Henry Wells and William G. Fargo also founded another of Buffett's top holdings, American Express (discussed in Chapter 5).

Buying a company experiencing serious business problems requires knowing a great deal about it and being confident the problems are temporary. For individual investors it may be advisable to buy a turnaround candidate only as part of a much more diversified portfolio.

Buy Stocks in Plummeting Markets

In May 1997, while on a whirlwind book tour, Katherine Graham stopped off in Omaha. She was there to listen to the speeches of Buffett and Munger at Berkshire Hathaway's annual meeting and to promote her book *Personal History.* A long line of Berkshire Hathaway shareholders had gathered, waiting to get the autograph of the woman who had enriched their pocketbooks by serving at the helm of The Washington Post.

According to The Washington Post's fact brochure, journalist Stilson Hutchins founded The Washington Post in 1877. A few others owned the Post and subsequently, it was sold to Eugene Meyer, a financier. Meyer's daughter Katherine married Philip Graham, a bright, charismatic man whom Meyer admired. When Meyer passed away, Philip took over, and in 1961, he bought Newsweek.

Raised in an era when few women worked and a woman's role was to take care of the home, Katherine Graham was thrust into running the Post as well as raising her children alone because of the death of Philip, at age 48, in 1963. The Post went public in 1971, selling for $26 a share. Between 1973 and 1974, the Dow Jones plummeted over 45 percent. During this time, the Post's coverage of the Watergate scandal received national attention. Reporters Bob Woodward and Carl Bernstein were busily writing stories about the Watergate break-in and the corruption in the White House that lead to President Nixon's resignation. When the Post's stock dropped 30 percent, Buffett bought, paying $6.37 a share (adjusted for splits). At the time, based on the company's revenues (sales), the Post's value was about four times the price he paid.[3] Buffett was impressed with the financial numbers as well as the integrity and quality of the people at the Post, including Katherine Graham, her editor Ben Bradley, and reporters Bob Woodward and Carl Bernstein.

Over the years, Buffett became an advisor and friend to Katherine Graham. Buffett served on the board of directors and because of his recommendations the Post instituted a program of buying back its shares and increased shareholder value in other ways.[4] In 1993, the year Katherine Graham retired, Buffett's investment in the Post of about $10 million was producing $7 million in dividends and had a market value of over $400 million. The 1999 year-end market value was $960 million.

Katherine Graham was elected by *Fortune* magazine to the Business Hall of Fame. Under her leadership the Post was awarded Pulitzer Prizes and she won accolades from both Buffett and Munger. Katherine's son, Donald, is now chairman of the Post.

The Evolution of Buffett's Strategies

As a youngster, Buffett studied technical analysis (technical analysts rely heavily on volume and price changes as opposed to evaluating a company's financial strength and profitability). Buffett even wrote an article for *Barron's* about odd-lot statistics, considered an unreliable technical indicator today. Then, Buffett read *The Intelligent Investor* by Benjamin Graham and was so impressed he traveled to New York where he studied security analysis with Graham. Years later, in 1994, speaking at a luncheon held by the New York Society of Security Analysts to honor Graham, Buffett remarked, "If I hadn't met Ben Graham, I might still be fooling around with the odd-lot statistics." Graham taught Buffett a different way of thinking about investing and became his mentor, teacher, employer, and hero.

When Graham went shopping on Wall Street, he was looking for stocks selling at bargain prices based on earnings or book value. Considered the father of value investing, Graham focused on the financial numbers of a company. To protect against purchases turning out to be lemons instead of bargains, Graham bought broadly diversified portfolios of stocks and bonds. Like one would wear a belt with suspenders for added protection, Graham bought stocks below what he thought they were worth, creating a Margin of Safety (a concept Graham developed). If Graham thought a stock was worth $20 a share and he could buy it at $14 a share, for example, the Margin of Safety would be 30 percent. The higher the Margin of Safety, the more comfortable Graham felt.

In the early years of Buffett's investment career, emulating Graham, he purchased well-diversified portfolios of stocks at statistically cheap prices. Going beyond Graham's teachings, Buffett has evolved as an investor, but still adheres to his mentor's core principles. Buffett's investments are more concentrated. He buys top-quality, well-run companies and is willing to pay more. For the most part, Graham sold stocks within a few years of purchase. Now, Buffett invests for the long term because he has found short-term investing doesn't provide the large profits an outstanding investment can over time.

Charlie Munger, vice chairman of Berkshire Hathaway and Buffett's partner and friend, has given him insights about buying great companies. Buffett also visited California money manager Phil Fisher, a pioneer of growth investing who concentrates more on the qualitative side of investing, judging the capability of management and how a firm is run. Buffett studied Fisher's investment approach and has applied some of his criteria for evaluating people, policies, and products of companies. An admirer of Fisher, Buffett has praised his investment skills at Berkshire Hathaway's annual meetings. Applying both Graham's concept of value investing and Fisher's approach for buying outstanding growth stocks, Buffett has combined growth and value strategies to create his own investment style.

Buffett's Commonsense Investment Rules

Investing takes discipline, patience, and knowledge, but it is also important to apply common sense. The following are eight of Buffett's commonsense rules for investing:

1. Have a written or mental note of your investment plan and have the discipline to follow it.

2. Be flexible enough to change or evolve your investment strategies when sound judgment and conditions warrant change.

3. Study sales and earnings of a company and how they are derived.

4. Focus on your purchase candidate. Understand the firm's products or services, the company's position in its industry, and how it compares with the competition.

5. Learn as much as possible about the people managing the business.

6. When you find a great stock value, don't be swayed by predictions for the stock market or the economy.

7. Sit on the sidelines in a cash position if you can't find investments of value based on your criteria. Many emotional investors make the mistake of buying at very high prices relative to value.

8. Define what you don't know as well as what you do know and stick to what you know.

Chapter 2

Buffett Applies the 3 Steps: Getting Insights from Annual Reports

Step 1. Gather the Information

To find investment leads and gather information about companies, Buffett reads publications such as *The Wall Street Journal, The New York Times, The Washington Post, Buffalo News, Forbes, Fortune, USA Today, Barron's,* and *Financial World.* He looks for news about potential purchase candidates, the industries in which they operate, and general economic conditions.

Buffett studies the operating history of a company to get an understanding of where it has been, as well as its current operations, which gives him clues as to where it may be headed. He reads his purchase candidate's company reports, which includes the annual, 10-K, 10-Q, and 8-K reports. The 10-K is an annual report required by the Securities and Exchange Commission (SEC) that contains much of the same information found in a company's annual report but provides additional details. The 10-Q is filed with the SEC quarterly and updates information to annual reports. The 8-K is used to report significant changes; for example, sales of assets or resignations of officers or directors.

Additionally, Buffett reads proxy statements, which solicit shareholders' votes for the board of directors or for other matters; list com-

10 K – annual report

10 Q Quarterly updates

8 K changes

pensation, stock ownership, and stock options of executives and directors; and contain comparative stock performance graphs. To help him compare backgrounds and financial track records of companies, Buffett studies competitors' reports as well.

Company reports can be obtained by calling or e-mailing investor relations departments, visiting the company Web sites (www.companiesonline.com contains the Web site addresses of many firms) and the Web site of the Securities and Exchange Commission (www.sec.gov). Names of competitors can be found through stock data research services and may be provided by investor relations departments.

A subscriber to *Value Line Investment Survey* (valueline.com), Buffett considers this a valuable research service for obtaining stock information. Other print and electronic stock data services also provide extensive stock data, such as Bloomberg Financial (www.bloomberg.com), Standard & Poor's (www.standardandpoor.com), and Morningstar (morningstar.com). Hoover's offers profiles of company histories (www.hoovers.com).

Buffett also may speak with management, competitors, and other people related to or knowledgeable about stock purchase candidates, and he often researches products by using them himself.

Step 2: Evaluate the Information

Buffett starts his evaluation by looking at a business to determine whether it meets his criteria. Then, he looks at the stock price to decide if it is attractive. Equating purchasing a stock to buying a piece of a business, Buffett asks questions such as:

- Is the business understandable?
- Are the CEO and top executives focused and capable based on the firm's previous track record of sales and earnings and how the business is run?
- Does management report candidly to shareholders?
- Does the company have top-quality, brand-name products used repeatedly and high customer loyalty?
- Does the company have a wide competitive edge and barriers to potential competition?

free cash flow

- Is the business generating good owner earnings—free cash flows?
- Does the business have a long-term history of increasing sales and earnings at a favorable rate of growth?
- Has the company achieved a 15 percent or better return on shareholders' equity and a return that compares favorably with alternative investments?
- Has the company maintained a favorable profit margin compared with the competitors' profit margin?
- What are the goals of the business and the plans to achieve them?
- What are the risks of the business?
- Does the business have good financial strength with low or manageable debt requirements?
- Is the stock selling at a reasonable price relative to future earnings and price potential?

Reading company reports and Value Line's research reports helps Buffett determine whether a company meets his criteria. A company may not meet all Buffett's expectations, but it has to be truly outstanding and selling at an attractive price.

Investment Insights from Annual Reports

Since 1956, when he began his career, Buffett has become a whiz at reading annual reports as well as other company reports. The difficult part for many investors is reading and understanding the financial statements. This may be overcome by reading the statements along with research reports that present the financial numbers in a more accessible manner, such as *Value Line Investment Survey* (covered in Chapter 3).

Reading Coca-Cola's annual reports helped Buffett make his decision to accumulate the stock between 1987 and 1988. Coca-Cola's annual reports gave Buffett information about management's goals and the firm's great growth potential in world markets.

Annual reports can reveal a potentially profitable investment or a company to avoid. When a Berkshire Hathaway shareholder asked Buffett, "How do you read annual reports?" Buffett replied, with a smile, that he reads them from cover to cover. The annual report starts with the CEO's letter to shareholders, then goes on to the financial highlights, a description of the business, management's discussion of the results of past operations, business segments including new products that may have been introduced, R&D activities, goals, and performance numbers. Next is the auditor's opinion and the financial statements. Back pages of the report contain the location and phone number of the corporation, Web site address, notice of annual meeting, and other information.

As Buffett reads the CEO's letter and management's discussion, he questions whether this is a report with valuable information for shareholders or primarily promotional material. Buffett expects the management of firms he buys to report openly and honestly.

Buffett's annual reports to Berkshire Hathaway's shareholders have been candid. In the 1976 annual report, Buffett remarked that he was disappointed in the textile division (subsequently sold). He explained that costs were high because management did not evaluate capabilities of equipment and employees properly. Berkshire Hathaway's 1994 annual report had a section called "Mistake D Jour." Buffett reserved top honors for his purchase of USAir preferred stock. The dividend was omitted September 1994 and the stock dropped. USAir is no longer held by Berkshire Hathaway.

Great investors are not immune to having some years when their stocks are down and the market is up. In 1999, the Standard & Poor's 500 Index increased 19 percent, but Berkshire Hathaway fell 15 percent. "Even Inspector Clouseau could find the guilty party; your Chairman," Buffett wrote in the annual report. Among Buffett's stock holdings, Coca-Cola was $58 at the end of 1999 down from its closing price of $67 in 1998; Gillette closed 1999 at $41, off from its 1998 close of $47. Both stocks fell further in early 2000. Over the long term these stocks have had good performance—Buffett's investment in Coca-Cola of $1.3 billion grew to $11.65 billion and his investment in Gillette of $600 million increased to $3.95 billion (as reported in Berkshire Hathaway's 1999 annual report).

One way to evaluate executives of a company is to read management's previous years' commentary about the company's goals, earnings, and other performance numbers in annual reports and compare them with the actual results. It is advisable to read annual reports for several years. Statements, such as "Our performance has added value to our shareholders," have to be put into perspective with whether sales and earnings shown on the financial statements are higher than the numbers for previous years.

Understand the Business

Buffett looks for businesses he understands with good economics. The annual report describes the nature of the business, how sales and earnings are created, and the firm's products or services. For example, in its 1998 annual report, Gillette's management described its business as the world's leader in sales of grooming products—blades, razors, and shaving preparations for men as well as selected shaving products for women. As of 1998, Gillette had a 69 percent market share of worldwide sales of razors and blades.

In 1996, Gillette acquired Duracell, the leading manufacturer and marketer of alkaline batteries. This gave Gillette a product that was a good fit for the business and made economic sense because of the company's already established worldwide distribution capability. Gillette's products are distributed in over 200 countries. Other products include Braun household appliances; Oral-B toothbrushes and oral care appliances; Parker, Papermate, and Waterman writing instruments; and Right Guard and Soft and Dri toiletries.

Gillette's financial reports show that earnings per share increased steadily from $0.31 in 1988 to $1.27 in 1998.

Corporate Goals and Plans to Achieve Them

Before making an investment, Buffett asks: *"What could go right? What could go wrong?"* Analyzing the goals, strategies, and risks of the business provides some answers.

An example of what could go right, Coca-Cola's goals include producing quality products priced relative to value; increasing sales volume by expanding beverage sales worldwide; and maximizing long-term free cash flow, earnings per share, and return on shareowners' equity.

To achieve its goal of increasing sales worldwide, Coca-Cola invests in production facilities, distribution networks, equipment, and technology in developed nations as well as in nations with developing (emerging) economies, such as China, India, and others. In the 1997 annual report, Coca-Cola's management illustrated the great potential for expansion of profits, comparing U.S. consumption rates of Coca-Cola beverages to consumption in lesser-developed nations. The annual report showed that the U.S. population of about 272 million has a per capita consumption of 376 eight-ounce servings a year. China, with over a billion people, has a per capita consumption of only six eight-ounce servings a year, and India's population of about 960 million has a per capita consumption of only three eight-ounce servings a year. That leaves a tremendous amount of room for growth.

Capital Resources and Liquidity

Corporate executives also discuss capital resources and liquidity in their annual reports, to show that their company is financially strong and capable of carrying out the firm's business strategies to achieve goals. Working capital, the money available to pay current obligations, is the difference between current assets and current liabilities. Current assets are assets that can easily be converted into cash (usually within a year) and include cash, marketable securities, accounts receivables, and inventories. Current liabilities are liabilities coming due within a year or less, such as bills, notes, taxes, and currently maturing debt. Generally, a ratio of $2 (or at least $1) of total current assets to $1 of total current liabilities is considered good, but this varies from company to company and industry to industry. The numbers to calculate working capital are found on a firm's balance sheet and in stock research reports in print or online.

The amount of working capital needed also depends on a firm's total sales, how rapidly inventory is turned over and accounts receivables are collected, and overall financial strength. Coca-Cola has reported negative working capital. A substantial company like Coca-Cola, however, with fast inventory turnover, easily collectible accounts receivables, and good cash flows can operate with much lower working capital than firms that don't meet these standards. For smaller or less financially strong firms it is usually more important to have higher working capital.

In the 1997 annual report, Coca-Cola's management explained the company's philosophy about working capital: "Our company maintains debt levels considered prudent based on our cash flow, interest coverage, and percentage of debt to capital. Credit ratings are AA from Standard & Poor's and AA3 from Moody's and the highest credit rating for our commercial paper programs. We raise funds with a low effective cost. Our debt management policies, in conjunction with our share repurchase programs and investment activity, typically result in current liabilities exceeding current assets."

Benefits of Buying Back Shares

Coca-Cola, Gillette, and many other companies have a strategy of buying back their shares, which may be discussed in their annual reports. When a company repurchases its own shares, it is reducing the amount of outstanding shares so that each shareholder has a larger portion of the earnings. To simplify this, if a firm with 10 million shares outstanding earns $10 million, per share earnings would be $1 a share; if the same firm had 5 million shares and earned $1 million, earnings would be $2 a share. Generally, it is a positive sign and a good strategy when a corporation buys back its shares.

The value of buying back shares, however, is predicated on the price the company pays for the shares and its future earnings.

Business Risks

In addition to presenting a view of where the company is headed, management provides cautionary statements, discussing risks that might affect the company's future. If risks of the business are not fully discussed in a firm's annual report, these risks should be covered in the firm's 10-K and quarterly reports.

Companies can experience business problems and earnings setbacks that make goals more difficult to achieve. Coca-Cola derives 75 percent of its profits outside North America and about 60 percent of Gillette's earnings come from international markets. Operating in the emerging markets of Asia and Latin America carries economic and political risks. Foreign currency rate fluctuations are also a risk. Plummeting currencies, such as seen with the Chinese yuan, Mexican peso, and Russian ruble, can contribute to lower earnings for multinational firms. Managers of Gillette and Coca-Cola use hedging techniques to reduce this risk, but may not always be successful. There is a risk that future demand for products might weaken, partially depending on whether advertising, marketing, and promotion are effective. In addition, competitive products may cut into profits and costs of raw materials needed for production of products may increase.

In Coca-Cola's 1994 annual report, former CEO Roberto Goizueta wrote: *"We have little control over global economic trends, currency fluctuations and devaluations, natural disasters, political upheavals, social unrest, bad weather, or schizophrenic stock markets. We do, however, have complete control over our own behavior, an accountability we relish."* This can apply to corporate executives as well as investors. From 1998 to early 2000, his words rang true as the firm encountered slowing profits due to weak global markets, a strong dollar, and other problems. In 2000, Coca-Cola announced employee layoffs and plans to restructure the company.

The Auditors' Report

A company can be a bad investment and still merit a clean opinion from auditors. The job of the auditors is to review evidence presented by management to support financial numbers and notes to financial statements. They determine if the statements follow generally accepted accounting principles (GAAP). Auditors may issue an unqualified or clean opinion, a disclaimer of opinion due to a limitation on the scope of the audit, or an adverse opinion, which is rare but occurs when auditors believe the statements do not represent the company's financial numbers accurately.

Buffett would advise serious investors to have a basic understanding of financial statements, the balance sheet, the income statement, and the statement of cash flows, as well as the principles of accounting. Although in-depth analysis of financial statements is beyond the scope of this book, Chapter 9 has some information about this subject.

Buffett's application of Step 2 and Step 3 continues in the next chapter.

Chapter 3

Buffett Applies the 3 Steps (continued): Getting Insights from Stock Research Reports

BUFFETT SUBSCRIBES TO the *Value Line Investment Survey* (valueline. com), available in print or electronic versions.

Value Line's reports are divided into sections by industry, with an overview page discussing the industry's outlook, current news about the industry, and composite statistics for sales, earnings, return on shareholders' equity, profit margins, debt, dividend yields, and other data. Company reports have a description and general commentary about the business, long-term performance numbers, projected earnings, and more. The *Value Line Investment Survey* format gives investors the ability to look at an entire group of stocks in one industry and compare the financial numbers of companies within that industry as well as an individual firm's current and past financial numbers. Using the soft drink industry reports, for example, Buffett can compare Coca-Cola with PepsiCo, Cadbury Schweppes, Cott, and others. As he studies these reports, Buffett pays close attention to long-term trends in sales and earnings, return on shareholders' equity, profit margins, and other numbers.

When using more than one stock data service, be aware that financial ratios may be calculated in different ways. Value Line, for example, calculates the operating profit margin of a company before depreciation (covered later), which gives a conservative view of this ratio; some stock research services include depreciation. It is important when making year-to-year comparisons of financial numbers of a firm to use the same ratio calculations. Buffett evaluates a stock as a business, so he would look at the total numbers as well as the per share numbers. For illustrative purposes, per share numbers are shown for Coca-Cola and Gillette in the following descriptions.

Look for a Track Record of Growing Sales and Earnings

Buffett doesn't search for stocks with spectacular performances that shoot up like a rocket and can fall just as quickly. He looks for solid growth and he buys stocks with the intention of holding them for at least ten years. So, he has to feel relatively comfortable about the firm's profit potential for the next ten or more years.

Companies Buffett purchases have a history of consistently increasing sales and earnings. The past, of course, is no guarantee of the future, but Buffett can be somewhat more comfortable about future predictability with firms that have a history of growth and stability.

Looking at the table below showing earnings from 1990 to 1998 for two companies, A and B, it should be obvious which company Buffett would prefer.

Year	Company A Earnings	Company B Earnings
1990	$0.40	*d$4.09
1991	0.49	*d 8.85
1992	0.58	*d 4.85
1993	0.67	2.13
1994	0.79	6.20
1995	0.93	7.28
1996	1.11	5.72
1997	1.28	7.89
1998	1.27	5.24

Source: *Value Line Investment Survey*
*d deficit

Company A is a stock Buffett owns, Gillette. Earnings were in an uptrend for most of the 1990s. In 1998 and 1999 (not shown in this table), however, Gillette suffered an earnings slowdown, in part due to the global economic weakness in 1997.

Company B, which shall remain nameless, had three deficits in the last ten years—1990, 1991, and 1992—as well as erratic earnings. Buffett has bought firms with earnings setbacks, but only when he perceived their problems to be temporary and the firm had a previous track record of success, which Company B has not demonstrated. Based on his investment philosophy, Buffett would avoid Company B.

Owner Earnings and Free Cash Flows

An investment mantra of Buffett's is "Just show me the cash—owner earnings." He buys firms generating earnings that can be used to grow the businesses—cash cows as opposed to capital-intensive companies that consume cash, such as mining companies requiring tremendous amounts of capital just to maintain equipment.

The standard calculation for cash flow, a popular measure used in conjunction with earnings, is net earnings per share plus depreciation per share, a noncash deduction from earnings to allow for wear and tear or obsolescence of equipment and other assets.

Buffett uses a similar calculation, adding depreciation per share to net earnings per share, but he also subtracts capital spending per share, which is the expenses required to maintain and upgrade plants and equipment. He calls this calculation owner earnings.

Cash Flow = Net Earnings Per Share + Depreciation Per Share
Owner Earnings = Net Earnings + Depreciation − Capital Spending

The figures to calculate owner earnings, cash flow per share, and capital spending per share are reported by Value Line for many companies and also can be found in annual reports.

Buffett's formula for owner earnings is sometimes referred to as free cash flows. This represents cash that managers can spend at their discretion in a variety of ways, such as researching and developing new products, advertising and marketing, and repurchasing the firm's stock. Generally, when calculating free cash flows, in addition to subtracting capital spending from cash flows, investors also subtract the cash dividend paid to shareholders. Although dividends are discretionary, investors usually anticipate receiving some dividends from companies that have a history of paying them. To calculate free cash flows using Value Line's numbers, subtract the dividend from Buffett's formula for owner earnings. Below is an example of the figures for Coca-Cola. For a more detailed explanation of free cash flows, see page 79.

1998 Owner Earnings and Free Cash Flows for Coca-Cola

Cash Flows	$1.70
Capital Spending	$0.50
Owner Earnings	$1.20
Minus Dividend	$0.60
Free Cash Flows	$0.60

Source: *Value Line Investment Survey*

Look for Favorable Profit Margins

It's a basic business principle, the more costs and expenses there are to deduct from sales, the less profits (earnings) there are for owners of a business. Buffett expects corporate executives to be conscientious about keeping costs under control.

At age six, Buffett got his first taste of profit margins. The profit margin shows the relationship between sales and earnings and can be calculated by dividing net income (after tax earnings) by sales, expressed as a percentage. Buffett bought Cokes from his grandfather's grocery store at 25 cents a six-pack and sold them for 30 cents a six-pack. Because his profit was 5 cents, and costs and taxes were zero, his net profit margin was about 16.6 percent (5 cents divided by 30 cents), which was quite good.

$$\text{Net Profit Margin} = \frac{\text{Net Income}}{\text{Sales}}$$

The profit margin may also be calculated based on a firm's operating earnings, which are earnings from the firm's main business as opposed to income from other sources such as from investments. Value Line's calculation for the operating profit margin is operating earnings before interest, depreciation, and taxes, divided by sales, expressed as a percentage.

$$\text{Operating Profit Margin} = \frac{\text{Operating Earnings before Interest, Depreciation, and Taxes}}{\text{Sales}}$$

Current profit margins should be compared to a company's past years' margins.

Profit margins should also be compared to competitors' margins. For example, Coca-Cola's profit margins have been much higher than its nearest competitor, PepsiCo. In 1998, Coca-Cola had an operating profit margin of 29.8 percent and a net profit margin of 18.8 percent; PepsiCo had an operating margin of 18.4 percent and a net profit margin of 7.9 percent. PepsiCo has spun off unprofitable divisions and changed the way it does business with bottlers to make it more efficient, so future profit margins may be higher.

Because profit margins vary from year to year and from industry to industry, it is also advisable to look at composite statistics for an industry when evaluating a firm's profit margins. Robert Morris Associates publishes the RMA *Industry Surveys,* which give expanded industry ratios. An investor also can obtain an overview of an industry using Value Line's industry composite statistics, which are less extensive.

1998 Profit Margins for Various Industries

	Operating Profit Margin	Net Profit Margin
Soft Drink Industry	20.0	8.0
Retail Stores	8.0	2.9
Groceries	7.1	2.4
Newspaper Industry	21.5	8.0
Machinery	13.5	5.8

Source: *Value Line Investment Survey*

Follow the Trend of Book Value

Book value, also referred to as shareholders' equity or the net worth of a business, is a theoretical number indicating what shareholders might receive if a firm were liquidated.

To calculate book value, subtract all liabilities (what the firm owes) from total assets (what the firm owns). When calculating book value, also deduct the value of preferred stock, an issue of stock that has a claim on assets before common stock. To calculate book value per share, divide the book value by the number of shares outstanding. Value Line reports book value. In annual reports, book value is listed as shareholders' equity (on a company's balance sheet).

$$\text{Book Value Per Share} = \frac{\text{Assets} - \text{Liabilities} (- \text{Preferred Stock})}{\text{Number of Shares Outstanding}}$$

In the mid-1950s, Buffett bought stocks selling close to or below book value per share and sold when his stocks advanced to prices above book value per share, a strategy successfully applied by Benjamin Graham. Years later during a 1993 speech he gave at Columbia, Buffett mentioned an outstanding example. He bought Union Street Railway of New Bedford, Massachusetts when it was selling at $45 with $120 a share in cash.

Today, Buffett views book value differently. He evaluates book value over a period of years to determine the trend—if book value is increasing or decreasing—which can be equated to tracking personal net worth. Coca-Cola's book value has grown from $1.18 a share in 1989 to $3.41 in 1998, and Gillette's book value has increased from $.09 a share in 1989 to $4.03 in 1998.

Pay Attention to Return on Shareholders' Equity

Buffett considers return on shareholders' equity (ROE), which is net income divided by shareholders' equity, one of the most important measures of a company. This ratio indicates how well corporate executives are managing the money invested by shareholders.

$$\text{Return on Shareholders' Equity} = \frac{\text{Net Income}}{\text{Common Stock Equity (Net Worth)}}$$

Generally, ROE of 15 percent or more is considered good, but this return should be compared with a company's ROE for previous years and with alternative investments. Investors also look at return on total invested capital (ROI) along with ROE (explained on page 138). Among Buffett's holdings in 1998, Gillette's ROE was 31.4 percent and Coca-Cola's ROE was 40.5 percent.

Buffett seeks to buy firms with consistently higher earnings, much of which are retained and reinvested wisely to create high returns. He has stayed away from firms with high expenses and low ROEs.

Buy Companies with Reasonable Debt

Shakespeare said, "Neither a borrower nor a lender be." Buffett might agree with him on a personal level, but wise use of debt can be productive for businesses. One way to evaluate debt is by looking at the debt-to-capital ratio. The capital of a company may be defined as the total value of its bonds or other long-term debt, preferred stock, and common stock. The debt-to-capital ratio used by many investors, as well as services such as Value Line, is actually a modified version of the sum of the capital. To calculate this ratio, divide long-term debt by long-term debt plus shareholders' equity (expressed as a percentage).

$$\text{Debt to Capital Ratio} = \frac{\text{Long-Term Debt}}{\text{Long-Term Debt} + \text{Shareholders' Equity}}$$

The numbers to calculate this ratio can be found in a firm's annual report. Debt is considered reasonable if a company's debt-to-capital ratio is about 33 percent or less. That is not to say, however, that debt over 33 percent is never reasonable because debt varies from company to company and from industry to industry, and depends on the policies of the firm's executives for use of the debt. As of the second quarter of 1999, Value Line reported Gillette's debt-to-capital ratio at 34 percent, which would be considered reasonable, and Coca-Cola's debt-to-capital at 8 percent, which is very low.

Debt has to be evaluated by looking at the purpose, interest rate paid, sales and earnings of the firm, as well as other considerations. During times of rising interest rates, companies with low or manageable debt will not suffer as much as firms heavily dependent on debt.

Variations on the Price-Earnings Ratio

Buffett has cautioned that investors who buy great companies selling at high price-earnings ratios can get hurt in the short term but should do well in the long term. However, this does not mean investors should pay excessively high price-earnings ratios for stocks. The price-earnings ratio (P/E), which is a stock's price divided by earnings per share for the past 12 months, is referred to as the trailing P/E. This ratio indicates how much investors are willing to pay for each dollar of a company's earnings per share and how optimistic they are about the future. In addition to the trailing P/E, Value Line reports P/Es that are calculated with the earnings from the past 6 months and projected earnings for the next 6 months. Value Line also provides the relative P/E, which is a firm's P/E in relation to all stocks followed by the service.

When Buffett bought Coca-Cola in 1988, it had a P/E of about 13 based on Value Line's calculation. Even though the average P/E for the 1,700 stocks followed by Value Line was 11, Buffett felt that the stock was attractively priced based on future potential. In 1998, Coca-Cola earned $1.42 a share. The high price was approximately $89 (a P/E of 52), and the low price was about $54 (a P/E of 39).

In a favorable market climate, investors are generally willing to pay more. P/Es are higher when inflation and interest rates are low, the economy is growing, and money is flowing into the market. In 1999, with inflation very low, the P/E of the Standard & Poor's 500 Index climbed to over 36. In the late 1940s and between 1974 and 1981, when inflation was high, the P/E of Standard & Poor's 500 Index was as low as 7.

High Inflation Lower P/E

Investment Returns and Company Growth Rates

Investors measure the performance of an investment by the average annual compounded rate of growth. The growth rate can be measured for sales, earnings, cash flows, and dividends of a company and is typically calculated and evaluated for five- and ten-year periods. A company's average annual compounded growth rate can then be compared to that of other companies and to a stock market index.

To illustrate comparing the performance (growth) of an investment to a stock market index, suppose an investor buys a stock for

$10,000 and ten years later it is worth $33,000. During the same period, the Standard & Poor's 500 Index (S&P 500 Index) increased at an average annual compounded rate of 10 percent. How did this investment's performance compare with that of the S&P 500 Index?

The answer can be calculated with simple math and a compounding table, or with a calculator or computer that has a compounding feature. First, find the compounding factor, determined by dividing the ending value of the investment ($33,000) by the beginning value ($10,000). The result is 3.3. Next, look at the table of compound interest factors that follows; find the number of years the investment was held (10) and go across that line to the closest number to 3.3 (3.4). Then, find the corresponding interest rate at the top of the table (13 percent). The investment in this example beat the S&P 500 Index, which grew at 10 percent (a $10,000 investment would have been worth approximately $25,937).

Compound Interest Factors

Interest Rate	10%	13%	15%	16%	17%	18%	19%	20%	25%
Years									
5		1.6	1.8	2.0	2.1	2.2	2.3	2.4	2.5	3.1
10		2.5	3.4	4.0	4.4	4.8	5.2	5.6	6.2	9.3

The growth rate of a company's earnings can be calculated in a similar manner. If a company's earnings for the past five years were

- Year 1: $3.20
- Year 2: $3.90
- Year 3: $4.15
- Year 4: $5.25
- Year 5: $6.50

divide the ending value ($6.50) by the beginning value ($3.20), and the result would be a compounding factor of 2.0. Looking at the next table, the result would be a compounded growth rate of 15 percent for five years.

Compound Interest Table

Interest Rate	10%	13%	<u>15%</u>	16%	17%	18%	19%	20%	25%
Years									
<u>5</u>		1.6	1.8	<u>2.0</u>	2.1	2.2	2.3	2.4	2.5	3.1
10		2.5	3.4	4.0	4.4	4.8	5.2	5.6	6.2	9.3

A company's earnings growth rate can be compared to that of industry competitors. Earnings growth rates of the past few years can also be compared to the growth rate of the past five or ten years.

Step 3: Make the Decision

By the time Buffett makes buying decisions, he has evaluated the risks as well as the potential profits and tested a company against his criteria. To review questions Buffett might ask regarding his criteria, see page 13. Buffett compares an investment he is considering buying to other stock purchase candidates as well as to alternative investments. In Chapter 4, the brief history of GEICO along with the application of Buffett's criteria to make this purchase provides further information about his decision-making process.

The Crystal Ball: Projecting Future Earnings and Stock Prices

Some investment professionals estimate the value of a company's stock by projecting future cash flows for a period of five or ten years, determining a residual value, and using a discount factor to determine the present value. The resulting figure is divided by shares outstanding to obtain a value per share. This method is complex and its usefulness for individual investors is questionable (except for very experienced investors). Although Buffett agrees with the concept, he has indicated that he does not formally project future cash flows. Besides, with Buffett's super mathematical ability, he could probably project future cash flows in his head.

Other investment professionals estimate future earnings of a company and the price of its stock using the firm's current earnings per share, a projected growth rate, and a P/E at which the stock might sell. The caveat is that sales or earnings growth rates for the next five or ten years may not be the same as the rate(s) projected and no one knows for sure at what P/E a stock will sell in the future, unless there is a crystal ball that really works. Professional as well as nonprofessional investors can be wrong in their estimates. Conditions that may throw business projections off are unexpected negative changes in global or domestic markets and specific business problems. Stock prices may fall due to the general stock market or investors' perception of a stock's value.

Buffett estimates his purchase candidate's probable earnings and potential stock price for the next ten years as well as his potential return on the investment. Based on what Buffett has said, he pays close attention to a firm's historical track record of owner earnings, return on shareholders' equity, and sales and earnings. Buffett looks for companies with a track record of stable sales and earnings growth, which helps somewhat in predicting its future. He has bought outstanding companies producing products used repeatedly that maintain a high-perceived value by customers. He also analyzes a firm's capability to distribute products domestically and internationally to determine how this might translate into future sales and earnings. Buffett doesn't try to pinpoint future earnings and stock prices, but he does attempt to estimate numbers that might be in the ballpark. There is a description of a quick method to estimate a company's future earnings and stock price at the end of Chapter 31.

For added protection, he applies Ben Graham's principle called the Margin of Safety and buys stocks selling at a discount to Buffett's own projection of the company's worth per share. Having as much knowledge as possible about purchase candidates and using conservative assumptions helps create a reasonable possibility that projected earnings may be in the vicinity of actual future results.

Holding and Selling Stocks

After Buffett buys stocks, he continues to monitor his holdings against his buying criteria. Regardless of earnings setbacks, Buffett will hold a stock he has bought for the long term if he believes the firm will continue to have good earnings growth in the future. And he may use wide market fluctuations in the stock or the general market as opportunities to buy more shares.

Although Buffett buys stocks he plans to hold for at least ten years and his favorite holding period coincides with his favorite life expectancy—forever—this does not mean he never sells sooner. Buffett may sell a stock to raise cash for an investment that he thinks is a much better value or if he decides a company no longer meets his criteria. The potential tax bill for selling a profitable stock shouldn't drive economic decisions, but it should be a consideration. When selling a stock, Buffett would want to replace it with one that he perceives has greater potential, after paying capital gains taxes and selling costs.

Chapter 4

GEICO Revisited

BUFFETT HAS BOUGHT insurance firms in property/casualty and related businesses, such as General Re, GEICO, National Indemnity Company, and Kansas Bankers Surety Company. One reason he likes insurance firms is that they offer the potential of very low cost capital. The float, which refers to funds derived from policyholders' premiums that remain with an insurance company until claims are paid, can be invested and the returns compounded.

When policy owners pay premiums for insurance, they receive a promise of a future payment in the event they have a claim covered by the policy. The type and amount of coverage depends on the terms and conditions of the insurance policy. The company may pay covered claims, as well as the costs of doing business, from premiums and income earned on investment holdings. Several factors determine whether an insurance firm will be a success. One is pricing and the perceived value of policies by consumers. Other factors are the quality of underwriting, control of expenses, strength of advertising and marketing, and ability to invest premium dollars profitably and maintain appropriate reserves.

Well known for selling auto insurance directly to consumers, GEICO was a public company until 1995, but is now privately held by Berkshire Hathaway. Many Buffett followers are aware that he first heard about GEICO in 1950, while studying at Columbia, when he learned that his professor, Benjamin Graham, was on the board of directors. His curiosity piqued, Buffett traveled to GEICO's headquarters in Washington, D.C., and met Lorimer Davidson, chief investment officer of the firm. He spent several hours questioning Davidson about the company and subsequently bought the stock. About a year later, Buffett sold his shares at a profit. It was not until several decades later, when GEICO was in a crisis, that Buffett began purchasing shares again and ultimately bought the entire company.

Today, GEICO is a strong well-known brand name, but years ago, in 1976, the firm was reporting losses and its stock had crashed from $60 to $2. To many investors, GEICO was in bad financial straits and recovery was uncertain. To Buffett, it was an ideal turnaround candidate. Investors buy companies experiencing serious problems when they think there is a good probability that the firm will recover financial health. The challenge of buying a turnaround candidate is to determine whether problems are temporary or if there is permanent irreversible damage.

Buffett knew that GEICO had the goodwill of customers, a recognized name, an exceptional CEO, and a prior track record of growing sales and earnings. Knowing the history of a firm in this type of situation as well as the state of its current operations is important as illustrated in the following history of GEICO along with the application of Buffett's criteria.[1]

Criteria: A Focused, Detail-Oriented CEO and an Understandable, Profitable Business

In 1934, with the U.S. economy still suffering from the Great Depression, Leo Goodwin started GEICO. Goodwin had been employed by a Texas-based company that sold automobile insurance to commissioned military officers. He had originally been an outside accountant for this firm and was asked to join the company. An intelligent, ambitious man, he learned the insurance business, worked in various capacities, was promoted to general manager, and hoped to become president. But Goodwin was informed that the firm would only allow a retired military officer to serve in that capacity and he didn't qualify. So, Goodwin decided to go into business for himself, even though he had been advised the odds of failure were high.

At the same time, Cleaves Rhea, president of a finance firm in Fort Worth, wanted to buy an auto insurance company to expand his operations. After meeting Rhea, Goodwin gave him details of a business plan he had developed to sell automobile insurance by mail to federal employees and some noncommissioned officers rated as good drivers.

Goodwin proposed to offer a deep discount from standard rates and provide top-quality service. By dealing directly through the mail, the cost of commissioned insurance agents would be eliminated. The business would have low overhead costs and little or no competition, as well as excellent potential for good profit margins and return on the money invested. Here was a simple, but great business concept. Rhea agreed to put up a substantial part of the money required to back the company and GEICO was founded in Fort Worth on March 20, 1934. Determined to make the business a success, Goodwin and his wife, a former bookkeeper, worked hard, long hours from early morning to late evening. As the discounts and excellent service GEICO offered attracted many policyholders, the company began to grow. Goodwin advertised in government employee publications around the country. Responses from the Washington, D.C., area were so high that Goodwin and Rhea decided to relocate there, which proved advantageous to GEICO because many government workers located in Washington, D.C., eventually became policy owners.

In 1947, Rhea decided to sell his share of the business. To help him find a buyer, Rhea called on Lorimer Davidson, who worked for a stock brokerage firm. One of the potential buyers Davidson met was Benjamin Graham. Although Graham had reservations about insurance companies as investments, he saw the great value and tremendous potential GEICO offered. Deciding the price was right, based on the financial numbers and future profit potential, Graham bought Rhea's interest. At the time, Graham was unaware that his firm, set up as an investment partnership, was prohibited by securities regulations from owning more than 10 percent of an insurance company. As a result, Graham had to distribute GEICO's stock to his investors and GEICO became a publicly traded company. A dividend paying policy was established. Graham joined the board of directors and Davidson became chief investment officer.

Criteria Applied: *Both Buffett and his mentor, Benjamin Graham, recognized the value of GEICO, with its low expenses, good profit margins, and excellent long-term profit potential. Goodwin is an example of the type of corporate leader Buffett seeks out: highly focused, intelligent, energetic, and determined to make the business a success.*

Criteria: An Outstanding CEO, Excellent Employee Relations, and Growing Sales and Earnings

In 1958, Goodwin retired and Davidson took over as president, subsequently becoming chairman. Davidson, a very gregarious man, was accessible to employees as well as executives. Creating a team spirit, he fostered employee involvement, instituting annual sporting events and starting a company club to participate in projects with charities. He encouraged employees to share ideas for improving service, efficiency of operations, or other concepts that might benefit the firm. Monetary bonuses were awarded for the best ideas. Eligibility for GEICO's car insurance was expanded to include private-industry professionals as well as other workers, and GEICO prospered as policyholders were added.

In 1965, Graham retired from the board of directors. Five years later, Lorimer Davidson retired from active management, but remained as a director. Under Davidson's leadership, the number of policyholders tripled, premiums written climbed from $40 million to more than $250 million. GEICO became the sixth-largest (stock) automobile insurance company in the United States.

Criteria Applied: *Davidson created excellent employee relations as well as higher sales and earnings. He met Buffett's criteria by being focused and candid, and by producing outstanding profits.*

Criteria: An Exceptional, Results-Driven, Candid CEO, and a Turnaround Stock Candidate with Great Potential

After Davidson stepped down, profits dropped and reserves fell for the first three quarters of 1970. Subsequently, two other CEOs ran GEICO under extremely difficult conditions. A number of internal and external events converged to throw GEICO into a crisis. Eligibility requirements for policyholders were lowered further. The company was expanding so quickly that the underwriters had trouble keeping up with the volume of new business. No-fault insurance laws, passed by many states, increased auto insurers' exposure to padded claims. Part of GEICO's surplus was invested in common stocks, and the Dow Jones Industrial Average plunged more than 45 percent between 1973 and 1974. In addition, high inflation caused higher auto repair and medical costs.

GEICO reported a substantial loss; capital was seriously depleted and reserves dangerously low. The dividend was omitted. In 1976, GEICO stock, which had traded around $60 a share three years before, crashed to $2 a share.

To combat the problems, GEICO executives instituted stricter underwriting requirements. The acquisition of new business was reduced and in some cases stopped, the common stock portfolio was sold, and a committee was appointed to find a new CEO.

During this time, John J. Byrne was executive vice president of Travelers Insurance Company. Byrne had helped Travelers create the company's first variable annuities. He was responsible for successfully turning around Travelers auto and homeowners business in 1974, after the firm had incurred severe losses. GEICO executives approached Byrne about taking over as CEO. After several meetings, he agreed to accept the challenge of restoring GEICO to financial health.

Byrne devised a plan to pull the company out of its troubles and took over with the tenacity of a wartime general. He tightened underwriting requirements further, imposed vigorous cost controls, replaced ineffective executives, and made wide cutbacks in the customer base through cancellations and nonrenewals. Temporary relief was provided through a reinsurance plan and capital needed was raised through underwriting an issue of convertible preferred stock.

In 1977, Byrne informed shareholders: "We executed the plan to turn GEICO around. The objectives have been met. Our company ended 1976 with approximately $137 million of surplus for the protection of policyholders and we managed to achieve a net income in the fourth quarter of approximately $8 million." Within three years, GEICO was showing a profit of more than $220 million. The stock began moving up and about a decade later it was selling more than $60 a share.

In 1980, during a speech Byrne gave for the Newcomen Society, he commented, "The story of GEICO from its early beginning, its years of growth, its brief period of financial adversity, and its great recovery epitomizes the best traditions of the Free Enterprise System."

Criteria Applied: *Byrne was candid, capable, and focused. Buffett knew that although GEICO was in financial trouble, the company still had the goodwill of its customers and a well-known name. He recognized Byrne as an exceptional CEO who had the potential to solve the company's problems. Investors, who sold out of fear, drove the stock down from about $60 to $2. At this point, Buffett stepped in and started buying, taking advantage of a great opportunity. He made subsequent purchases. About 20 years later, Buffett's Berkshire Hathaway acquired the whole company, paying $70 a share for the remaining shares. Buffett's purchase of GEICO is an example of buying an extraordinary turnaround candidate.*

GEICO is now under the leadership of Lou Simpson and Tony Nicely. An excellent money manager, Simpson manages the investments. Nicely oversees the underwriting. Having been with the firm for many years, Nicely is a conservative underwriter by training and experience. Run by these outstanding men, GEICO has achieved solid growth and is an outstanding brand name.

Chapter 5

Applying Buffett's Strategies for Different Types of Investors

IN ADDITION TO owning quality bonds and cash equivalents, conservative investors who buy individual stocks can apply Buffett's criteria and buy brand-name companies such as those that have been among Buffett's holdings. Of course, doing so depends on the price of the stock and the condition of the company at the time of purchase. Other examples of industry leaders with brand-name recognition that may meet Buffett's criteria are General Electric, Procter & Gamble, Johnson & Johnson, FDX (formerly Federal Express), Home Depot, Office Depot, Morgan Stanley Dean Witter, Merrill Lynch, and Wal-Mart.

Moderate or aggressive investors could own the same type of stocks Buffett buys, as well as other types of stocks within their comfort zones that meet his criteria. Some investors have modified and applied Buffett's criteria for buying established technology companies. Generally, however, technology firms are subject to rapid change, products can become obsolete quickly, and barriers to competition may be low. This makes long-term earnings of these companies less predictable than the type of firms Buffett buys. Diversifying among technology stocks and companies with more predictable futures can help protect against losses. Aggressive investors might want to apply a modified version of

Buffett's criteria to smaller firms and attempt to find lesser-known companies that may become tomorrow's household names.

Investors who want professional management can buy Berkshire Hathaway, as well as purchase a mutual fund, or hire a money manager who uses similar criteria to Buffett's. The fund or private money manager should have a proven, long-term track record of success. The track record should be studied year by year, comparing the numbers with an appropriate index, such as the S&P 500, and peer group performance. Consideration should be given as to what the real return for past performance would have been after taxes, fees, and expenses. For mutual funds, it is important to read the prospectus and the statement of additional information to learn about the fund's objectives, fees and expenses, and track record. Read annual and quarterly reports to find out what stocks the fund has owned.

Chapter 6

The Ultimate
Annual Meeting

IN 1998, AFTER Berkshire Hathaway's annual meeting, I gave a talk at the Omaha Press Club, recapping the speeches of Buffett and Charlie Munger. The following description of this meeting (based on my speech) gives a general idea of how Berkshire Hathaway's annual meetings are run and provides further advice from Buffett and Munger.

Although the meeting officially started at 9 AM, shareholders arrived in droves at the Aksarben Stadium as early as 6:30 AM to make sure they got good seats. (Annual meetings are currently held at the Omaha Civic Auditorium.)

As is the custom, before entering the main room where the meeting is held, shareholders encountered an array of booths with product displays from many of Berkshire Hathaway's holdings. In addition to being a great investor and businessman, Buffett is also a great marketer. Disney employees dressed as Mickey Mouse and other favorite characters surrounded Disney CEO Michael Eisner (Buffett sold Disney in 1999). GEICO was set up to give quotes on auto insurance policies. Berkshire's own booth was buzzing with activity, as Buffett and his daughter Susie stayed there for a while before the meeting started.

At 8:30 AM a film clip was shown, a tradition for the last several meetings. The film clips are spoofs of Buffett and Munger. There was a short dialogue depicting Buffett as "Citizen Buffett," a take-off on the movie *Citizen Kane*. In the film, when asked the secret of investing, Buffett answered, in essence, buy at the lowest price and hold forever. Lorimer Davidson gave a brief summary of the GEICO story as it related to Buffett. When the film ended, Buffett and Munger walked out on the stage to the thundering noise of enthusiastic audience applause.

Within a half-hour, the business part of the meeting was over and for the next six hours Buffett and Munger answered questions from shareholders. Questions came from youngsters as well as seniors, varying from how stocks are chosen to the future of the market. Buffett pointed out that the stock market had posted unprecedented returns, companies had reported record earnings, and interest rates were low. To determine the direction of the market, he said that investors have to ask themselves if this will continue indefinitely.

Silver, ROE, and Internet Stocks

The media had drawn attention to Buffett's purchase of silver, bought in 1996, but Munger remarked that the purchase represented only 2 percent of Berkshire Hathaway's assets. Buffett again emphasized the importance of return on shareholders' equity and buying stocks at the right price, a discount to value. He commented on Internet stocks that have no earnings and sell at lofty prices. Buffett said that if he were teaching a class on security analysis, there might be a question on the final exam requiring students to determine a value for these Internet stocks. If any of the students did, they would fail.

A lady sitting toward the back of the auditorium asked Buffett about his health, referring to his consumption of candy, ice cream, and other such treats. Buffett responded quoting the late George Burns. When Burns was in his nineties, someone asked him what his doctors thought about his smoking. Burns replied that his doctors were dead.

"What keeps you up at night?" a young woman asked Buffett. He explained that he sleeps well because as problems arise he addresses them.

Buying Back Shares and the Cost of Stock Options

In response to another question, Buffett commented on stock buy-backs, which are fashionable with corporate managers. He pointed out that buying shares at unjustifiably high prices doesn't build shareholder value.

Buffett also spoke about stock options. Stock options can be costly to shareholders, but aren't listed on the income statement as an expense; if exercised, these options dilute earnings. Buffett believes that a better way to compensate managers is to give them a cash bonus based on performance, which they can use to buy their firm's stock outright.

A few questions came from high school students. Buffett recommended that they start a savings and investment program as soon as possible, get a good business education, and learn how excellent businesses are run.

At 3:30 PM, the meeting ended. Although the crowd had thinned out, some shareholders said they could have stayed all day and were already planning their trips for next year's meeting.

Chapter 7

The Life and Career
of Warren Buffett

BUFFETT WAS BORN on August 30, 1930. Times were tough. It was the Great Depression and Buffett's father, a stockbroker, struggled to find customers and earn a living.

As a youngster, he began gaining expertise that would help him understand the workings of a business and its stock. At age six, he bought six-packs of Coke from his grandfather's grocery store for 25 cents and resold them for 30 cents. Even at that young age, he saw the consumer appeal of Coke. Years later in 1985, Buffett made Cherry Coke the official drink of Berkshire Hathaway. In 1988, he began buying Coca-Cola's stock and became its largest shareholder.

Buffett's father was elected to Congress in 1942, and the family moved to Washington, D.C. Continuing his money-making pursuits, Buffett delivered newspapers for *The Washington Post*. When he bought its stock in 1973 and became the second-largest shareholder, he could say that he previously worked for the paper.

While attending high school, Buffett also engaged in other business ventures. One of the most profitable was buying pinball machines and installing them in barbershops. By the time he graduated from high school, Buffett had earned about $10,000 (over $100,000 in today's dollars). Buffett attended Wharton and transferred to the University of Nebraska, graduating in 1950.[1]

Buffett's Early Investments

After reading *The Intelligent Investor* by Benjamin Graham, Buffett decided to attend Columbia University (where Graham was teaching) so he could study with him. To Buffett, Graham was much more than a teacher: Graham was his hero. In 1954, he worked for Graham's firm. Walter Schloss, who also worked for Graham, recalls that they used manuals such as Standard & Poor's stock guides to search for bargain-priced stocks. In 1956, Graham closed his business and moved to California where he could continue teaching and writing. Schloss went into his own business as a money manager and now works with his son, Edwin. Armed with Graham's teachings and the confidence that he would be a big success, Buffett returned to Omaha to begin managing money. He started an investment partnership and became general partner, with family members and others who invested with him as limited partners.

Born in Omaha, Charlie Munger graduated from Harvard law school and moved to California. During one of Munger's trips to visit family members still living in Omaha, he met Buffett. Munger became Buffett's friend and partner. A brilliant man who can get right to the heart of a matter with few words, Munger shares the stage with Buffett at Berkshire Hathaway's annual meetings and occasionally gives his insights.

Buffett's early investments were much like Graham's. For example, one stock Buffet bought, Union Street Railway of New Bedford, Massachusetts, selling for about $45 with $120 cash per share, is the type of bargain Graham would buy. In 1963, Buffett invested in American Express. That year, a subsidiary of American Express (no longer in existence) gave receipts to a small oil-refining firm in exchange for tanks thought to contain vegetable oil. There was a problem, however, because the tanks were filled with seawater. The refining firm declared bankruptcy, leaving American Express with hundreds of millions of dollars of debt and a negative net worth.

As the stock of American Express fell from $65 to $35, Buffett saw an investment opportunity and bought. He recognized that the company still had the goodwill of customers and a continuing stream of cash from credit cards and travelers checks. Buffett didn't buy this stock on financial numbers; he bought it based on his judgment that American Express had a well-known brand name, loyal customers, and the ability to weather this storm.

Prior to the scandal, American Express had undergone a reorganization, making it more efficiently run. In addition, senior officials called on bankers across the country to make sure they knew how determined the firm was to remain solvent and continue to grow. Sales of travelers checks and credit cards increased substantially the following year.[2] American Express rebounded and Buffett profited.

In 1965, Buffett acquired control of Berkshire Hathaway, a firm that made fabrics for home use, such as drapes. The price he paid was less than the working capital (current assets minus current liabilities) of the firm. Although Buffett realized profits from Berkshire, he later sold the firm's equipment at a price much lower than book value. He ultimately turned Berkshire Hathaway into a highly successful holding company—a vehicle used to buy stocks and private businesses.

Toward the end of the 1960s, the stock market became overheated and speculation was rampant. Buffett could no longer find stocks that met his criteria and he was worried about a major market correction. In a letter to his partners, Buffett informed them that he was liquidating the partnership. He offered them the choice of taking cash or continuing to hold Berkshire Hathaway and a few other stocks. His timing was right. During the bear market crash of 1973 and 1974, doing business as the chairman of Berkshire Hathaway, Buffett acquired outstanding investments (covered in the beginning of Part I) and subsequently continued on the path that would take him to the top of the investment world.

Buffett's Speeches

Today, Buffett shares his wisdom, speaking at annual meetings, writing his annual reports, and giving lectures to high school and college students. Because they are young and in their formative years, his advice can help students by shaping their ideas about business and investing. He stresses the importance of getting a good business education, learning how excellent companies are run, and building a financial foundation by establishing a pattern of saving money early in life. Citing his own experience, Buffett points out that the money he saved as a youngster went into buying stocks.

Perhaps someone in his audiences will turn out to be another Warren Buffett. In the meantime, there is only one Buffett and he has a phenomenal long-term track record of investment success!

PART II

Benjamin Graham: The Value Numbers Investor

You can beat the market and there's more than one way to win on Wall Street. Benjamin Graham and his disciples proved it. The Einstein of investing, Graham invented and developed formulas and principles. However, instead of applying his theories to energy and matter like Einstein, Graham used investment criteria to test the value of a company and its stock.

During his college years, Graham was offered teaching positions in English, math, and philosophy at Columbia. But with guidance from his dean and to help his family as well as himself financially, Graham went to work for a Wall Street firm, taking a path with potential for far greater wealth. After establishing a reputation as an outstanding money manager, Graham returned to Columbia to teach security analysis and become Wall Street's best professor.[1]

Known as the father of security analysis and creator of value investing, Graham also wrote several books. His writings and teachings provided a foundation for other investors to build on. John Templeton studied with Graham and refers to him as "the great pioneer of security analysis." To Warren Buffett, Graham was mentor and role model. George Nicholson, a founder of the National Association of Investors Corporation (NAIC), was influenced by Graham's writings and incorporated some of his principles into NAIC guidelines. Money manager Martin Zweig, who combines fundamental and technical investing, applies a modified version of Graham's investment criteria.

Harry Markowitz, winner of the Nobel Prize in economics in 1990 for his dissertation on asset allocation, read one of Graham's books, later met him, and now applies an expanded version of the value style.[2]

Soon after Graham began working on Wall Street in 1914, rampant speculation and manipulation of stocks became commonplace. Stock market operators bought large blocks of stocks and circulated rumors, such as unfounded reports of earnings increases, enticing other investors to buy these companies. Then, when the stocks went up high enough, they dumped their shares, leaving gullible investors with losses. This was legal prior to the establishment of the Securities and Exchange Commission in 1934.[3]

Graham brought ethics as well as logic and reason to the investment field. Today, he would likely advise investors only to use Web sites of reputable stock data services for research on the Internet and to gain a good understanding of the companies they are buying.

When Graham went shopping on Wall Street, he was looking for quality merchandise on sale—undervalued stocks primarily based on earnings and assets. The many professional money managers and individual investors who follow Graham's philosophy have expanded or fine-tuned his investment criteria, but still adhere to his timeless core investment principles.

Chapter 8

Graham's Success Strategies: The Cornerstones of Investing

GRAHAM STARTED HIS career working in the bond department of a brokerage firm. His job was evaluating the safety of bonds and deciding if a firm issuing bonds was creditworthy. Studying a company's ability to pay interest and principal based on stability and growth of earnings, book value (assets minus liabilities), amount of debt, and other criteria gave him a good background for analyzing stocks. Graham's experience coupled with his outstanding ability in math led him to emphasize the quantitative aspect of companies—financial numbers. But he was aware of the importance of management and that any changes taking place within the company, its industry, or the general economy could affect the future of a business.

Value, Growth, or a Combination of Both

Graham's investment approach has become known as value investing. Generally, value investors buy stocks at low prices relative to per share earnings, sales, or book value and apply other criteria as well. Often, stocks that value investors buy have higher dividend yields than the average stock.

Growth stock investors, on the other hand, are willing to purchase stocks with lower dividend yields that are selling at higher prices in relation to per share earnings, sales, or book value. Typically, growth stock investors look for companies that report more rapid growth of earnings than the average company with higher perceived long-term profit potential.

Warren Buffett and others disagree with the notion that value and growth have to be separate. Seeking to buy growth stocks at value prices, Buffett looks at value and growth as being two sides of the same coin. As it turned out, Graham's biggest stock winner was GEICO, a great growth company now privately owned by Buffett's Berkshire Hathaway.

Different Interpretations of Value Investing

Just as no two stars in the sky are exactly alike, investors who follow Graham's approach and apply his core principles may use different criteria and own very different stocks. Graham did not own technology stocks, which frequently have erratic earnings and can be difficult to value. Money manager Chris Davis of Davis Selected Advisers considers himself a value investor; however, he has purchased Motorola, Texas Instruments, and Intel as well as other types of stocks. David Dreman of Zurich Kemper Management follows the value style and has bought financial stocks such as Fannie Mae, Bank America, and First Union, in addition to other kinds of businesses.

Among firms owned by Graham disciples John Spears and Chris and Will Browne, the managing directors of Tweedy Browne, are Kmart and American Express. Mason Hawkins of Southeastern Asset Management has purchased real estate–related companies like Marriott International and other types of businesses. Further details of how Spears and Hawkins apply Graham's strategies are covered later.

A Variety of Ways to Buy Undervalued Stocks

Graham bought unpopular, underresearched, out-of-favor stocks. He purchased stocks of small unknown firms and larger well-known, financially sound companies selling at bargain prices. Stocks might be selling at cheap prices due to a general market correction, the unrecognized value of a company by investors, and the actual or perceived business problems of a firm or an industry.

To protect against potential losers, Graham owned as many as 100 different stocks. Some professional money managers own broadly diversified portfolios and others concentrate their investments, holding many fewer stocks. Mason Hawkins, for example, owns 25 or 30 different issues in his mutual fund portfolios. The portfolios of John Spears consist of more than 100 stocks. Individual investors can have it both ways by owning a concentrated portfolio of between 10 and 20 stocks and also purchasing one or more mutual funds for greater diversification.

Graham's Core Investment Principles

In 1994, speaking at a luncheon of the New York Society of Security Analysts held to honor Graham, Warren Buffett said that Graham's core principles are the cornerstones of sound investing and will be as important 100 years from today as they are now:

- Use a Businesslike Approach to Investing.
- Buy stocks with a Margin of Safety.
- Be prepared to deal with Volatile, Irrational Markets.

Using a Businesslike Approach to Investing[1]

Watching the movement of the stock market, investors can easily forget that a stock represents a fractional ownership in a company, not just a certificate with frequent price changes. Graham advised investors to use a businesslike approach. This means to think of investing as buying a piece of a business. He taught the importance of studying financial reports of companies and justifying purchases with sound reasoning and logic.

Buying Stocks with a Margin of Safety[2]

Graham's emphasis was on avoiding losses. Depending on the size of a loss, it may be difficult just to break even. If an investor purchases a stock for $10,000 and the stock drops to a market value of $5,000 (a 50 percent loss), it takes a 100 percent increase to break even.

Lose 50 Percent	Get Back 100 Percent
$15,000	$7,500
– 7,500	+ 7,500
$7,500	$15,000

The table below shows varying losses with the percentage gains needed to break even.

Percentage Loss	Percentage Gain Needed to Break Even
–40%	+67%
–30	+43
–20	+25
–15	+18

To help cushion potential losses, Graham used a Margin of Safety— a simple, but important concept of investing. The Margin of Safety represents the amount at which an investor can buy a stock below his or her estimate of value. If Graham thought a stock was worth $20, and he could buy the stock at $14, his Margin of Safety would be 30 percent. The higher the Margin of Safety, the more protection on the downside and the greater the comfort level Graham would have. For further protection, he owned a variety of stocks in different industries and businesses as well as bonds.

Making Rational Decisions during Volatile Bull and Bear Markets

Knowing that the stock market is influenced by the emotions of investors, Graham stressed the need for rational thinking. Emotional control is especially important when the market becomes a raging bull, wildly optimistic as stock prices climb to lofty heights, or a ferocious bear, deeply depressed as prices plummet.

During bear markets, when stocks are very depressed, some investors panic and sell out. But to a value investor, a bear market can be a buying opportunity. Investing when the market is plummeting, however, is not always easy. It takes courage and discipline to invest at times when the outlook for stocks is gloomy, especially in prolonged bear markets.

A bear market is generally defined by investment professionals as a decline of 20 percent or more in a major stock market index. The next table shows time frames and percentage declines of 20th century bear markets for the Dow Jones Industrial Average, S&P 500 Index, and Nasdaq.

Dow Jones Industrial Average			Standard & Poor's 500 Index		
Start	*End*	*Loss (%)*	*Start*	*End*	*Loss (%)*
06/18/01	11/09/03	−46.1	09/09/29	06/01/32	−86.2
01/20/06	11/15/07	−48.6	07/19/33	03/14/35	−33.9
11/20/06	09/25/11	−27.4	03/08/37	03/31/38	−54.5
10/01/12	07/30/14	−24.1	11/10/38	04/28/42	−45.8
11/22/16	12/19/17	−40.1	05/31/46	05/17/47	−28.8
11/05/19	08/24/21	−46.6	06/16/48	06/13/49	−20.6
09/04/29	07/08/32	−89.2	08/03/56	10/22/57	−21.6
02/06/34	07/26/34	−22.8	12/13/61	06/26/62	−28.0
03/11/37	03/31/38	−49.1	02/10/66	10/07/66	−22.2
11/14/38	04/28/42	−41.3	12/02/68	05/26/70	−36.1
05/31/46	06/13/49	−24.0	01/12/73	10/03/74	−48.2
04/09/56	10/22/57	−19.4	09/22/76	03/06/78	−19.4
12/14/61	06/26/62	−27.1	12/01/80	08/12/82	−27.1
02/10/66	10/07/66	−26.2	08/26/87	12/04/87	−33.5
12/05/68	05/26/70	−35.9	07/17/90	10/11/90	−19.9
01/12/73	12/06/74	−45.1			
09/22/76	02/28/78	−26.9			

			Nasdaq Index		
04/28/81	08/12/82	−24.1	*Start*	*End*	*Loss (%)*
08/26/87	10/19/87	−36.1	12/31/68	05/26/70	−35.3
07/18/90	10/11/90	−21.2	01/12/73	10/03/74	−59.9
			02/11/80	03/27/80	−24.9
			06/01/81	08/13/82	−28.8
			06/27/83	07/25/84	−31.5
			08/27/87	10/28/87	−35.9
			10/10/89	10/16/90	−33.0

Starting and ending dates of bear markets for various years are different for these indexes because they consist of different stocks and may not move in sync.

Technically, a bear market decline is defined as a correction of 20 percent or more; however, there are some widely known bear markets included in these tables that are just under 20 percent. According to Bridge/CRB (Chicago, Illinois), the S&P 500 Index and the Dow Jones Industrial Average were down less than 16 percent, and the Nasdaq was off 19.6 percent in 1997.

Source: InvesTech Research

In the June 1999 semiannual report to shareholders of his mutual funds, Mason Hawkins expressed concern at a time when the market was wildly optimistic, during an extended bull market: "The persistently good investment environment has dulled even the bears' view of risk. Stocks have advanced from 1990 lows by approximately 465 percent, at a rate of 21.8 percent annually, with dividends reinvested."

Hawkins commented that the price-to-earnings ratio of the S&P 500 Index was 36 and dividend yields had become inconsequential to investors. "Frenetic day trading has grown to become a meaningful percentage of Wall Street's daily volume," Hawkins continued. "Internet IPOs are being floated with such frequency that most new student entrepreneurs believe any reasonable MBA.com idea should make them billionaires." Believing the risk for investors of losing money was high, Hawkins posed a rhetorical question, "How should we react to this unprecedented market environment?" His Graham-like answer was, in essence, that investors should have the discipline and patience to wait for the right buying opportunities, stick to the principles of value investing, and apply a Margin of Safety to purchases.

Invest Regularly Using Dollar-Cost Averaging[3]

A strategy Graham suggested for individual investors is to invest a fixed dollar amount at regular intervals, known as dollar-cost averaging. With this strategy, investors buy more shares of stocks or mutual funds when prices are low and buy fewer when prices are high. *Temporary price drops can be of benefit provided that when the investment is ultimately sold, the value is higher than the average cost. Reinvesting dividends on a regular basis is a form of dollar-cost averaging.*

In the following hypothetical example of dollar-cost averaging, the price at the start and end of the period was $10. The investor in this example would own 70.44 shares and the original $600 investment would be worth $704.40 at the end of the period.

An Example of Dollar-Cost Averaging

Month	Amount Invested	Price	Shares Purchased
January	$100	$10.00	10
February	100	12.00	8.33
March	100	8.25	12.12
April	100	6.00	16.6
May	100	7.50	13.33
June	100	10.00	10

Total Amount Invested: $600
Average Cost: $8.96
Total Number of Shares Purchased: 70.44
Current Worth: $704.40

Graham and His Followers Apply the 3 Steps: Going Bargain Hunting for Undervalued Stocks

Step 1: Gather the Information

To find leads and gather information about companies, Graham studied industry and company reports and used research services such as Standard & Poor's and Value Line. "Value investing is now easier and more fun than in the past," John Spears comments. "Technology has made it easier to analyze companies. We can point and click and surf the Internet for information. We can now look for investment ideas globally. There are over 10,000 publicly traded stocks in the United States and about that many abroad. Computer screening permits investors to take a universe of stocks and screen out those issues that do not fit in with their criteria."[1] With computer software programs, investors have the ability to screen stocks for specific criteria such as price-to-earning (P/E) ratios, earnings growth rates, profit margins, and return on shareholders' equity. Some computerized stock programs provide income statement and balance sheet numbers, as well as analysts' estimates of future earnings and buy or sell recommendations.

Standard & Poor's (www.standardandpoor.com), Value Line (valueline.com), Morningstar (morningstar.com), and other services sell software for screening stocks. The American Association for Individual Investors (aaii.com) and the National Association of Investors

Corporation (better-investing.org) also sell this type of software and offer members other educational materials. According to John Bajkowski, editor of *Computerized Investing,* a publication of the American Association for Individual Investors, "When choosing computer programs to screen stocks, investors should consider initial and ongoing costs, ease of using the software, type of data and number of stocks included in the program, criteria that can be applied, special features, and intervals between updates."

Step 2: Evaluate the Information

If Graham were investing today, some questions he might ask to determine if a stock qualified for purchase would include:

- Does the firm's earnings growth rate compare favorably with industry peers?
- Does the company have a long-term record of consistently growing sales and earnings?
- Are profit margins favorable and is the business reporting a good return on shareholders' equity?
- Is the debt low or reasonable?
- Does the company have an uninterrupted long-term record of paying dividends?
- Is the stock selling at a low or a reasonable price relative to earnings per share and/or book value per share?

Followers of Graham, who have modified and expanded his criteria, also might ask:

- Do the top executives own a significant amount of the company's stock?
- Are insiders buying a significant amount of the firm's stock?
- Is the company repurchasing its shares?
- Is the company generating strong free cash flows?
- Is there a catalyst to create higher earnings and spark investor interest, such as new products, policies, or markets?
- Is the stock selling at a low price relative to sales per share?
- Is the stock selling at a reasonable price in relation to future potential earnings?

Investment Guidelines and Exceptions

For the most part, Graham used a strategy of broad diversification and preferred to buy stocks paying dividends. His average holding period was about two years. But there were some exceptions. The most outstanding was his purchase of GEICO. Graham invested 25 percent of the assets of his business in GEICO, which was high based on his diversification policy. GEICO paid no dividend initially and Graham held it for over 20 years, much longer than his typical holding period.

When Graham purchased GEICO, it had characteristics of a value stock—attractive based on its earnings and book value. During the years he held GEICO, however, the stock sold at higher P/Es than Graham paid and it would be considered a growth stock.

Graham bought a 50 percent interest in GEICO for $720,000, which eventually grew to be worth over $1 billion dollars.[2]

Study Company and Industry Reports

Graham used company and industry reports like treasure maps to find valuable assets. In 1926, after reading Northern Pipeline's annual report and an Interstate Commerce Commission report, Graham discovered that the company owned bonds worth about $95 a share. According to Graham, there was no business reason for the company to own these bonds. Northern Pipeline was out of favor because competition was cutting into business and earnings were lower. The stock was selling at an attractive price, $65 and paying a $6 dividend. Graham decided to buy. Subsequently, he paid a visit to Northern Pipeline's management, pointing out that the company had no need for these bonds and the money represented by them really belonged to the shareholders. Eventually, due to his persistent efforts, Northern Pipeline sold its bonds and distributed $70 a share to shareholders, and Graham then sold the stock with a good profit.[3]

Evaluate Financial Statements

When studying financial statements in annual reports, Graham would ask, "Is the company strong financially and is it profitable?" To determine a company's financial health, he evaluated the balance sheet, analyzing the assets (what the firm owns), the liabilities (what the firm owes), and the difference, shareholders' equity (also referred to as book value or net worth). To determine the profitability of a company, he examined the income statement, studying sales, costs and expenses of doing business, and the bottom line—profits (earnings).

Contemporary investors also analyze a company's statement of cash flows. The statement of cash flows, which has been required since 1987 (Graham passed away in 1976), shows inflows and outflows of money for the period covered. Cash flows are divided into three categories: (1) operating, (2) investing, and (3) financing. Investors like to see both positive earnings and positive cash flows.

Notes to financial statements can be complicated and difficult to read, but it is worth taking the time to study them. In his book, *The Intelligent Investor*, Graham discussed a company that appeared to be attractive, with a P/E of ten. For the fourth quarter of 1970, this company reported earnings of $1.58, but notes to the financial statements showed unusual and questionable write-offs. Graham calculated the earnings as $0.70 and, after adjusting for these charges, the P/E was actually 22 instead of 10.[4]

Notes may contain information about changes in accounting methods, claims from lawsuits or lawsuits pending, environmental issues, expiration dates of leases, maturity dates of debt and interest rates paid on debt, extraordinary deductions, nonrecurring earnings, and changes in income tax rates.

What Ratios Can Reveal

Graham used financial ratios to help him determine the value of a company. Financial ratios express the relationship between numbers found on financial statements. For instance, profit margins relate sales to profits (earnings) and show how much each dollar of sales is being turned into earnings, as discussed in Chapter 3. This ratio indicates how efficiently management is running the company. The return on shareholders' equity (ROE) is a ratio that relates earnings to shareholders' equity. ROE indicates how well corporate executives are managing the shareholders' investment in the company. Financial ratios should be compared for a period of years to determine long-term trends and also compared with the same ratios of competitors.

Various ratios can be evaluated, but some are more important depending on the type of company. The inventory turnover ratio, for example, which shows the number of times inventory is turned over during the year, is important when evaluating a retail firm as opposed to a bank. At the end of this chapter there is a description of this ratio and many of the financial ratios Graham might apply (see page 66).

To decide if a stock was selling at a bargain price, Graham evaluated the P/E and the price-to-book value ratio.

The P/E and P/S

Although Graham was uncomfortable about buying stocks with high P/Es (stock price divided by earnings per share for the last 12 months), he didn't have hard and fast rules for this ratio. Early in his career, he was able to buy greatly undervalued groups of stocks with low P/Es. One stock bargain Graham mentioned in the first edition of the well-known book he wrote with coauthor David Dodd, *Security Analysis,* was Wright Aeronautical. The stock was selling for $8 a share, earning $2 a share, a P/E of 4; it had cash per share of $8 and paid a dividend of $1.[5]

In later years, Graham recommended that conservative investors limit P/Es to 20 for value stocks and also said that growth stocks could be bought with much higher P/Es; he left it to the judgment of his readers or students. Today, if a company with a high P/E reports disappointing earnings, Wall Street is likely to punish the stock and the price will drop. *Graham would advise that investors evaluate stocks with high P/Es carefully and have sound reasons for expecting future earnings to continue at a satisfactory rate of growth.* Knowing the difficulty of projecting earnings, Graham analyzed the earning power of a company based on the stability and growth of earnings for the previous ten years.

A caveat regarding P/Es is that a stock can have a very high P/E because the company is reporting no or little earnings, but may qualify for purchase if there is a sound reason to believe future earnings will be higher. In this case, investors look at other criteria including the price-to-sales ratio (P/S), a ratio used by value investors in more recent years. The P/S relates the stock price to sales per share. To calculate the P/S, divide the stock price by the sales per share. The P/S varies from industry to industry, but generally a stock selling with a P/S of under one would be considered attractive.

$$P/E = \frac{\text{Stock Price}}{\text{Earnings Per Share}} \qquad P/S = \frac{\text{Stock Price}}{\text{Sales Per Share}}$$

Compare Stocks with Earnings Yield

The earnings yield, a ratio used by Graham, is the flip side of the P/E. The earnings yield is calculated by dividing a company's earnings per share by the stock price, expressed as a percent. If a stock is selling at $10 a share, earning $1 a share, the P/E is ten and the earnings yield is 10 percent ($1 divided by ten). The earnings yield of a company can be compared with that of other companies, as well as with interest rates paid on bonds and by banks.

$$\text{Earnings Yield} = \frac{\text{Earnings Per Share}}{\text{Stock Price}}$$

Consider a Stock's Book Value

During the time Graham was investing, he could find many stocks selling at prices below book value per share. With the average stock of the S&P 500 Stock Index selling around five times book value in 1999, buying stocks at prices less than book value has become difficult. Stocks meeting this criteria may be available, however, during steep bear market corrections, among stocks of cyclical companies experiencing downturns, and stocks of smaller U.S. firms or international ones.

In 1991, John Spears bought Champion International, a manufacturer of paper products that owns timberland, at approximately 60 percent of book value. Spears explains his rationale, "The paper business was in the doldrums in 1991, paper prices were low, and the industry mired in recession." Spears says that although he didn't consider Champion a great business (due to its cyclical nature), he was willing to own this stock at an extremely cheap price with the intent of selling when the stock reached his price target. According to Spears, eventually paper prices firmed, Champion began to make money again, the stock went up, and he sold it with a good profit.[6]

To calculate a stock's price-to-book value per share, first determine the book value per share, which is assets minus liabilities plus the value of preferred stock, divided by the number of shares outstanding. Next, divide stock price by book value per share.

$$\text{Book Value Per Share} = \frac{\text{Assets} - \text{Liabilities} + \text{Preferred Stock}}{\text{Number of Shares Outstanding}}$$

$$\text{Price-to-Book Value Per Share} = \frac{\text{Stock Price}}{\text{Book Value Per Share}}$$

If a stock is selling at $10, for example, and book value per share is $10, the price-to-book value would be one. A stock selling at a book value of one or under would be considered a bargain. But a low price-to-book value may not be an indicator of value; it may indicate a company with deeply rooted problems, and stocks bought based on this criteria should be part of a broadly diversified portfolio. At various times, Graham purchased stocks at prices below book value, and even bought stocks for less than a company's net current assets per share (NCAV). The formula for NCAV is: current assets (assets that can be converted into cash within a year—cash equivalents, marketable securities, inventories) minus all liabilities (including long-term debt, preferred stock, or other liabilities) divided by the number of shares outstanding.

$$\text{NCAV} = \frac{\text{Current Assets} - \text{All Liabilities}}{\text{Number of Shares Outstanding}}$$

The NCAV doesn't take into consideration the value of fixed assets such as plants and equipment, making stocks that qualify really cheap, and also difficult to find. In 1997, however, Spears bought Franco Tosi, an Italian-based company, selling at less than half its net cash per share. Graham would have been impressed.

Price Ratios Comparisons

The P/E, P/S, or price to book can be compared to price ratios of a company's industry and a general stock market index. The following example shows the P/E, P/S, and price-to-book value per share for a consumer finance company. The price ratios for this company compare favorably with those of its industry and the S&P 500 Index. The current P/E of 14 compares favorably with the stock's five-year-high P/E of 52.1 and five-year-average P/E of 30.1 (average of 52.1 and 8.1).

An Example of Price Ratio Comparisons, Dec., 1999

Price Ratios	Company	Industry	S&P 500
Current P/E Ratio	14.3	20.3	31.4
P/E Ratio 5-Year High	52.1	28.0	38.8
P/E Ratio 5-Year Low	8.1	8.0	14.7
Price/Sales Ratio	2.14	2.45	2.16
Price/Book Value	3.09	4.22	5.11

Courtesy of MSN MoneyCentral (moneycentral.msn.com/investor)

Buy Brand-Name Companies at Discounted Prices

Value investors buy outstanding companies with great brand names, such as Johnson & Johnson, General Electric, or Merck, which may not be selling at low P/Es or low price-to-book value, but these stocks have to be selling at greatly discounted prices from their high of one year or more. This may occur because of a general market correction or a temporary business problem.

Most investors are intuitively aware that the price they pay for an investment and the performance determines the return, but they may not think of this in numerical terms. To illustrate, in 1992, Disney stock sold at a low of $9.50 and high of $15, adjusted for splits, and at the end of 1998, six years later, it was $30. An investor who paid $15 in 1992 would have had an average annual compounded return of about 12 percent (based on the price of $30 in 1998); an investor who paid $9.50 would have had an average annual compounded return of about 22 percent; and an investor who paid $12.24 (the average of the high and low prices) would have had an average annual return of about 16 percent.

The Cost of a Stock Affects an Investor's Potential Return

1992	Price Paid	1998 Price	Compounded Average Annual Return
Low	$ 9.50	$30	22%
High	15.00	30	12
Average	12.25	30	16

The Importance of Dividends

Investors put less emphasis on high cash dividends today than in Graham's time and believe companies can reinvest money otherwise paid out in dividends to create future growth. Graham recommended buying companies with a long-term uninterrupted record of growing dividends.

The dividend yield is a stock's dividend per share divided by the price. The dividend yield can be compared to yields of other stocks and to interest rates of bonds and money market accounts. But a stock's potential total return (appreciation plus the income from dividends) should be considered.

$$\text{Dividend Yield} = \frac{\text{Dividend Per Share}}{\text{Stock Price}}$$

The safety of a company's dividend is measured by how much of the earnings is being paid out in dividends. Historically, industrial companies have paid out 50 percent or less of their earnings per share, and utilities more. If the amount of dividends paid is too high, there may be a danger of a dividend reduction in the future. Dividend policies differ from company to company depending on the stability of earnings, management's business strategies, and the firm's financial needs.

Step 3: Make the Decision

Graham would not buy a stock unless he had sufficient information to make an intelligent decision and the firm met his criteria. (To review questions Graham would ask regarding his criteria, see page 58.)

Graham said that investors should have a well-thought-out reason for buying and selling stocks. He recommended having a definite selling policy, which would include both an estimated holding period and a reasonable profit objective.[7] Some investors who follow Graham's strategies keep stock shopping lists with predetermined target buying and selling prices.

Graham's average holding period was two years. His followers have different holding periods and selling guidelines. Mason Hawkins, for example, has an average holding period of five years, and Warren Buffett buys stocks planning to hold them for at least ten years.

The following is from an article about financial ratio analysis written by John Bajkowski, editor of *Computerized Investing,* for the *AAII Journal* (American Association of Individual Investors). Bajkowski has studied and written about Graham; his article covers financial ratios Graham might look at and relates to "What Ratios Can Reveal," page 60.

Financial Ratio Analysis: Putting the Numbers to Work[8]

Financial ratio analysis uses historical financial statements to quantify data that will help give investors a feel for a firm's attractiveness based on factors such as its competitive position, financial strength, and profitability.

Financial statement analysis consists of applying analytical tools and techniques to financial statements in an attempt to quantify the operating and financial conditions of a firm.

Ratio Analysis

Ratios are one of the most popular financial analysis tools. A ratio expresses a mathematical relationship between two items. To be useful comparisons, however, the two values must be related in some way. We have selected some widely used ratios that should be of interest to investors. As with all ratios, a comparison with other firms in similar industries is useful, and a comparison of these ratios for the same firm from period to period is important in pinpointing trends and changes. It is also important to keep in mind that these ratios are interrelated and should be examined together rather than independently.

Operating Performance

Operating performance ratios are usually grouped into asset management (efficiency) ratios and profitability ratios. Asset management ratios examine how well the firm's assets are being used and managed, while profitability ratios summarize earnings performance relative to sales or investment. Both of these categories attempt to measure management's abilities and the company's accomplishments. [Note: The explanations of these ratios are next, followed by examples of how to calculate them. Included are an example of a balance sheet and an income statement.]

Asset Management

Total asset turnover measures how well the company's assets have generated sales. Industries differ dramatically in asset turnover, so comparison to firms in similar industries is crucial. Too high a ratio relative to other firms may indicate insufficient assets for future growth and sales generation, while too low an asset turnover figure points to redundant or low productivity assets.

Whenever the level of a given asset group changes significantly during the analysis, it may help the analysis to compute the average level over the period. This can be calculated by adding the asset level at the beginning of the period to the level at the end of the period and dividing by two, or in the case of an annual figure, averaging the quarter-end periods.

Inventory turnover is similar in concept and interpretation to total asset turnover, but examines inventory. We have used cost of goods sold rather than revenues because cost of goods sold and inventory are both recorded at cost. If using published industry ratios for company comparisons, make sure that the figures are computed using the same method. Some services may use sales instead of cost of goods sold. Inventory turnover approximates the number of times inventory is used up and replenished during the year. A higher ratio indicates that inventory does not languish in warehouses or on the shelves. Like total asset turnover, inventory turnover is very industry specific. For example, supermarket chains will have a higher turnover ratio than jewelry store chains.

Receivables turnover measures the effectiveness of the firm's credit policies and helps to indicate the level of investment in receivables

The Balance Sheet: An Example

Assets

Current Assets		
Cash		$ 320
Accounts receivable	1,070	
Less: allowance for doubtful accounts	90	
Net accounts receivable		980
Inventory		1,400
Prepaid expenses		100
Total Current Assets		2,800
Investments		350
Property, Plant and Equipment		
Land, buildings, machines, equipment, and furniture	930	
Less: accumulated depreciation	230	
Net property, plant & equipment		700
Other Assets		
Goodwill		300
Total Assets		4,150

Liabilities and Stockholder's Equity

Current Liabilities	
Accounts payable	$540
Accrued expenses	230
Income tax payable	60
Notes payable	170
Current portion of long-term debt	100
Total Current Liabilities	1,100
Long-Term Liabilities	
Deferred income tax	150
Long-term debt	1,000
Total Liabilities	2,250
Stockholder's equity	
Preferred Stock	200
Common stock	600
Paid in capital	800
Retained earnings	300
Total Stockholder's Equity	1,900
Total Liabilities and Stockholder's Equity	4,150

needed to maintain the firm's level of sales. The receivables turnover tells us how many times each period the company collects (turns into cash) its accounts receivable. The higher the turnover, the shorter the time between the typical sale and cash collection. A decreasing figure over time is a red flag.

Seasonality may affect the ratio if the period ends at a time of year when accounts receivable are normally high. Experts advocate using an average of the month-ending figures to better gauge the level over the course of the year and produce a figure more comparable to other firms. When averaging receivables, most investors will have to rely on quarter-ending figures to calculate average accounts receivable.

Average collection period converts the receivables turnover ratio into a more intuitive unit—days. The ratio indicates the average number of days receivables are outstanding before they are collected. Note that a very high number is not good and a very low number may point to a credit policy that is too restrictive, leading to lost sales opportunities. Meaningful industry comparisons and an understanding of credit sales policy of the firm are critical when examining these figures.

Profitability

Long-term investors buy shares of a company with the expectation that the company will produce a growing future stream of cash or earnings even when investing in emerging industries such as the Internet sector. Profits point to the company's long-term growth and staying power. There are a number of interrelated ratios that help to measure the profitability of a firm.

Gross profit margin reflects the firm's basic pricing decisions and its material costs. The greater the margin and the more stable the margin over time, the greater the company's expected profitability. Trends should be closely followed because they generally signal changes in market competition.

Operating profit margin examines the relationship between sales and management-controllable costs before interest, taxes, and nonoperational expenses. As with the gross profit margin, one is looking for a high, stable margin.

[*Net*] *Profit margin* is the "bottom line" margin frequently quoted for companies. It indicates how well management has been able to turn revenues into earnings available for shareholders. For our example, about 4½ cents out of every dollar in sales flows into profits for the shareholder.

Industry comparisons are critical for all of the profitability ratios. Margins vary from industry to industry. A high margin relative to an industry norm may point to a company with a competitive advantage over its competitors. The advantage may range from patent protection to a highly efficient operation operating near capacity.

Return on total assets examines the return generated by the assets of the firm. A high return implies the assets are productive and well-managed.

Return on stockholder's equity (ROE) takes this examination one step further and examines the financial structure of the firm and its impact on earnings. Return on stockholder's equity indicates how much the stockholders earned for their investment in the company. The level of debt (financial leverage) on the balance sheet has a large impact on this ratio. Debt magnifies the impact of earnings on ROE during both good and bad years. When large differences between return on total assets and ROE exist, an investor should closely examine the liquidity and financial risk ratios.

Liquidity

Liquidity ratios examine how easily the firm could meet its short-term obligations, while financial risk ratios examine a company's ability to meet all liability obligations and the impact of these liabilities on the balance sheet structure.

The *current ratio* compares the level of the most liquid assets (current assets) against that of the shortest maturity liabilities (current liabilities). A high current ratio indicates high level of liquidity and less risk of financial trouble. Too high a ratio may point to unnecessary investment in current assets or failure to collect receivables or a bloated inventory, all negatively affecting earnings. Too low a ratio implies illiquidity and the potential for being unable to meet current liabilities and random shocks like strikes that may temporarily reduce the inflow of cash.

The *quick ratio,* or acid test, is similar to the current ratio, but it is a more conservative measure. It subtracts inventory from the current assets side of the comparisons because inventory may not always

The Income Statement

Net Sales Revenue	$8,500		Income After Taxes	430
Less Cost of Goods Sold	5,600		Extraordinary Gain (Loss)	15
Gross Income	2,900		Gain (Loss) on Discontinued Operations	(60)
Operating Expenses			Cumulative Effect of Change in Accounting	(5)
Selling, Administrative and General	1,600		Net Income	380
Research and Development	450		Less Preferred Dividends	10
Depreciation	80			
Amortization of Intangibles	20		Net Earnings Available for Common	370
Total Operating Expenses	2,150			
Operating Income (EBIT)	750		Common Dividends	100
Other Income (Expense)			Earnings Per Share—Basic	3.70
Interest Income (Expense)	(120)		Earnings Per Share—Diluted	3.66
Non-Operating Income (Expense)	50		Dividends per Share	1.00
Gain (Loss) on Sale of Assets	(10)		*Consolidated Statement of Retained Earnings*	
Total Other Income (Expense)	(80)		Balance, Beginning of Year	30
			Net Income	370
Income Before Taxes	670		Cash Dividend Declared on Common	(100)
Income Taxes	240		Retained Earnings Balance, End of Year	300

be quickly converted into cash or may have to be greatly marked down in price before it can be converted into cash.

Financial Risk

Times interest earned, or interest coverage ratio, is the traditional measure of a company's ability to meet its interest payments. Times interest earned indicates how well a company is able to generate earnings to pay interest. The larger and more stable the ratio, the less risk of default. Interest on debt obligations must be paid, regardless of

Financial Ratios

Operating Performance

Asset Management

$$\text{Total asset turnover} = \frac{\text{Net sales revenue}}{\text{Total assets}} = \frac{\$8,500}{\$4,150} = 2.0\text{x}$$

$$\text{Inventory turnover} = \frac{\text{Cost of goods sold}}{\text{Inventory}} = \frac{\$5,600}{\$1,400} = 4.0\text{x}$$

$$\text{Receivables turnover} = \frac{\text{Net sales revenue}}{\text{Net account receivables}} = \frac{\$8,500}{\$980} = 8.7\text{x}$$

$$\text{Average collection period} = \frac{365}{\text{Receivables turnover}} = \frac{365}{8.7} = 42.0 \text{ days}$$

Profitability

$$\text{Gross profit margin} = \frac{\text{Gross income}}{\text{Sales revenue}} = \frac{\$2,900}{\$8,500} = 34.1\%$$

$$\text{Operating profit margin} = \frac{\text{Operating income (EBIT)}}{\text{Sales revenue}} = \frac{\$750}{\$8,500} = 8.8\%$$

$$\text{[Net] Profit margin} = \frac{\text{Net income}}{\text{Sales revenue}} = \frac{\$380}{\$8,500} = 4.5\%$$

$$\text{Return on assets} = \frac{\text{Net income}}{\text{Total assets}} = \frac{\$380}{\$4,150} = 9.2\%$$

$$\text{Return on stockholder's equity} = \frac{\text{Net income} - \text{preferred dividends}}{\text{Common equity*}} = \frac{\$380 - \$10}{\$1,700} = 21.8\%$$

Liquidity and Financial Risk

Liquidity

$$\text{Current ratio} = \frac{\text{Current assets}}{\text{Current liabilities}} = \frac{\$2,800}{\$1,100} = 2.5\text{x}$$

$$\text{Quick ratio} = \frac{\text{Current assets} - \text{inventory}}{\text{Current liabilities}} = \frac{\$2,800 - \$1,400}{\$1,100} = 1.3\text{x}$$

Financial Risk

$$\text{Times interest earned} = \frac{\text{Operating income (EBIT)}}{\text{Interest expense}} = \frac{\$750}{\$120} = 6.3\text{x}$$

$$\text{Debt to total assets} = \frac{\text{Total liabilities}}{\text{Total assets}} = \frac{\$2,250}{\$4,150} = 0.5\text{x}$$

* Total stockholder's equity less preferred stock

company cash flow. Failure to do so results in default if the lender will not restructure the debt obligations.

The *debt-to-total-assets ratio* measures the percentage of assets financed by all forms of debt. The higher the percentage and the greater the potential variability of earnings translate into a greater potential for default. Yet, prudent use of debt can boost return on equity.

The Bottom Line

Financial ratio analysis relies on historical financial statements to study the past and develop a feel for a company's attractiveness measured through factors such as its competitive position, financial strength, and profitability.

Knowledge of financial ratios should give investors a feel for how a company might react to shifts in industry, financial, and economic environments.

Chapter 10

21st-Century Value Investing with John Spears and Mason Hawkins

How John Spears Applies Graham's Strategies[1]

Howard Browne, father of Chris and Will Browne, was Graham's stockbroker. Chris, Will, and John Spears, who are the managing directors of Tweedy Browne, now work closely together as a team. They manage two mutual funds and private accounts, applying Graham's principles with an expanded version of his criteria (the name of Spears is used in this book collectively for these three men who work closely together).

Using online data and computer software, Spears searches the universe of publicly traded companies for bargain-priced stocks selling at low prices relative to per share earnings, sales, book value, free cash flow, and price history. Spears also looks for companies with insider buying—the purchase of a company's shares by its directors, executives or other employees, and share buybacks (companies repurchasing their own shares).

Spears has owned large, well-known companies as well as smaller, lesser-known ones. His U.S. stock holdings have included Kmart, American Express, Coca-Cola Bottling, McDonald's, and Wells Fargo. Among international holdings have been Unilever of the Netherlands, Fuji Photo Film of Japan, and Christian Dior of France.

Spears diversifies broadly and may own over 100 different stocks. Based on the cost, no stock represents more than about 4 percent of the total portfolio and no industry accounts for more than 15 percent.

Questions to Ask Management

After narrowing down purchase candidates, Spears focuses on individual companies with the best investment potential. Spears studies current and past financial statements and calls top executives of purchase candidates with a list of the following questions:

- Are you comfortable with analysts' projections for your earnings?
- What is your outlook for selling more products and increasing prices?
- How will increases in prices and unit sales affect the bottom line (earnings) of your income statement?
- What is your outlook for earnings growth over the next five years and how will this be achieved?
- What are your plans for cash generated from earnings not paid out as a dividend?
- Have insiders bought or sold your stock recently and, if so, why?
- What are your projections for return on shareholders' equity?
- How will competition affect your company?
- Are you considering consolidations or mergers?

Bloomberg Financial (www.bloomberg.com) and Zack's Investment Research (zacks.com) provide analysts' earnings projections and other stock data. Investor relations departments and a firm's CFO or other executives may answer these types of questions. Insider buying is reported in services such as Thomson Investor Network (www.thomsoninvest.com), MoneyCentral (moneycentral.msn.com/investor), and Insider Trader (insidertrader.com).

Insider Buying

Frequently, companies that Spears buys are repurchasing their own shares, the firm's executives own a substantial number of shares, and there is a significant pattern of purchases by one or more insiders. Insiders sometimes buy their own company's stock when it is depressed because they have knowledge about something that could contribute to the increased future value of the business. They might be aware of new marketing programs, increases in orders for products, positive changes in industry conditions, potential earning power of the company once nonrecurring new product development costs stop, and other factors.

In 1997, United Dental was selling around $10, off from its high of $31. "Earnings had collapsed due to glitches in the firm's computer system," according to Spears. "But 1998 earnings were estimated at $1.23 a share and a number of company insiders were aggressively buying shares at or near $10. The dental HMO industry was fragmented and consolidation was occurring within the industry." Six months after Spears bought this stock, between $10 and $11 a share, another firm, Protective Life, announced a buyout of United Dental using cash and shares worth approximately $19.44 a share. "Takeovers are not an infrequent occurrence in deep value stocks," Spears comments.

Buying Brand-Name Companies That Stumble and Rebound

"One of the better businesses that we were able to buy cheaply and still own is American Express," Spears says. "We have owned shares in this company since 1990. Our initial shares were purchased at prices between $19 and $26 a share [the stock was $166 at the end of 1999]. When we first looked at it, the company was facing what appeared to be significant competitive pressure from Visa and MasterCard. Earnings were under pressure and the focus had shifted from the credit card franchise to building a financial supermarket. The stock was under pressure and nobody wanted to own it. We felt strongly that if the company once again focused on the credit card business, it would have normalized earnings power of roughly $2.00 to $2.50 a share. The stock was trading at eight to nine times what we felt it could and should earn over time. In 1993, Harvey Golub became CEO and dismantled the conglomerate, sold a number of businesses, and refocused on the business' core strengths. American Express has been increasing its earnings and compounding value for our clients as well as ourselves."

Beyond Book Value

Researching and evaluating a firm's assets can result in finding hidden assets. At times, Spears evaluates certain assets such as land and equipment, going beyond the stated value on the balance sheet. Plants and equipment, for instance, are reported on the balance sheet at cost less accumulated depreciation (land is reported at cost) and may be worth more or less than the numbers show.

To estimate the value of real estate, Spears has called real estate brokers or appraisers who are knowledgeable about the property. Prior to buying and profiting from the stock of a company headquartered in Miami, Florida, that owned 22 acres of land adjacent to Biscayne Bay, Spears spoke with a real estate broker in the vicinity. The broker advised that the land was worth four times the balance sheet value. Spears also considers the value of intangibles such as brand names and patents, and might call a firm's CFO to find out the approximate value of a significant asset.

Investing Sensibly

Spears buys stocks with understandable financial numbers. International stocks are purchased only in countries where Spears can get enough information and where political and economic climates are conducive to investing. Stocks that aren't found in Spears' portfolios are companies that rely on fad products or services, or businesses that are difficult to evaluate.

Inflation and Stocks

In the 1999 annual report to shareholders of Tweedy Browne's mutual funds, Spears wrote: "In the long run, one of the greatest risks to your net worth is not owning stocks. Bonds do not grow. They can only return their face value at maturity. Although inflation is currently at historically low levels, it still exists. Inflation is a silent, insidious tax that erodes your net worth. Within our lifetimes, having a million dollars was considered a fortune. Also in our lifetimes, college cost $2,500 a year, an expensive car cost $8,000, and $100,000 bought a luxurious house. Our grandparents can remember going to the movies for a nickel. One of the problems with living a long time is that your point of reference for the cost of something is cheaper. Fortunately, there is an easy way to keep pace with and even beat inflation, and this is stocks."

As to the future of value investing, Spears comments, *"We believe that the stock market in its excess will continue to undervalue and overvalue securities relative to intrinsic value."*

How Mason Hawkins Applies Graham's Strategies[2]

When he was in high school, Mason Hawkins received a gift of Graham's book, *The Intelligent Investor.* He found reading this book an enlightening experience that made a lasting impression. Creating a wonderful tribute to Graham, Hawkins gave a monetary grant to his alma mater, the University of Florida, to fund classes that teach practical applications of Graham's principles.

Hawkins' firm, Southeastern Asset Management, manages private accounts and four mutual funds. Two of his funds have been closed to new investors—one that invests in large and midsize companies and another that focuses on stocks of smaller companies. In addition, Hawkins manages a real estate mutual fund consisting of real estate–related companies and natural resource firms, as well as an international fund. The funds' top holdings have included FDX (formerly Federal Express), Marriott International, United Healthcare, Rayonier, Gulf Canada Resources, and Yasuda Fire and Marine Insurance of Japan.

Hawkins owns about 20 to 30 stocks in each of his portfolios. His first rule of investing is "buy a good business at an attractive price." To Hawkins, a good business is a company with a competitive edge, a strong brand name, low-cost production, and a dominant industry position. His goal is to buy stocks selling at a 40 percent discount to his estimate of value and sell when stocks reach his projected price. Hawkins' average holding period has been five years.

He studies company reports, interviews management, and uses *Value Line Investment Survey* and *Standard & Poor's Stock Reports* for secondary research. Hawkins also keeps a database of companies that have been acquired by other firms and the prices paid. Like looking at comparable sales when buying real estate, Hawkins uses the information to compare selling prices of purchase candidates to prices paid for similar firms.

Free Cash Flows and Capital Spending

An important financial indicator Hawkins looks at is free cash flows, which represents money executives can invest at their discretion in various ways: R&D, marketing and advertising, reducing debt, expanding operations, and repurchasing shares. If free cash flows are invested wisely over time, this should create higher earnings and ultimately be reflected in higher stock prices.

To calculate free cash flows, subtract capital spending per share from cash flow per share. Cash flow per share is net earnings to which depreciation (or other noncash deductions) has been added back because it is a noncash deduction. When calculating free cash flows, Value Line and other stock data services also subtract the cash dividend per share. The following table shows the calculation of free cash flows for Ralston Purina, a stock Hawkins bought then sold. In 1992, he began accumulating Ralston Purina at an average cost of $36.67 and sold it at $106 in 1998 (free cash flows are illustrated for 1998).

Free Cash Flows for Ralston Purina

Cash Flows Per Share:	$1.83
Capital Spending Per Share:	$0.74
Free Cash Flows before Dividend:	$1.09
Cash Dividend Per Share:	$0.40
Free Cash Flows after Dividend:	$0.69

Source: *Value Line Investment Survey*

Sometimes a firm may have low or negative free cash flows because it is making heavy capital expenditures in expectation of generating higher future free cash flows. Marriott International, a stock Hawkins has owned is an example. In 1998, Marriott had positive cash flows, but the company's capital spending was higher than its cash flow. Marriott's capital spending was being used for the development of living facilities for seniors and building other properties to be franchised. Management considered this spending as an investment that would produce strong free cash flows later.

According to the company's historic fact publication, Marriott started out in 1927 as a small root beer stand. Marriott grew to become a well-known owner of real estate, including hotels and other properties. Today, the company owns very little real estate, which is capital intensive. In its 1998 annual report, Marriott executives explained that their goal is to manage and franchise properties, which should produce substantial [free] cash flows, especially with the company's well-established brand name. By franchising properties, Marriott collects franchise payments and management fees. The franchisee pays capital expenditures and may also pay for the expense of building the hotel or other type of facility. Marriott has an agreement with franchisees to ensure hotel upkeep and service, and surveys customers to find out if quality service is being maintained. While some investors still thought of Marriott as a company that owned real estate, Hawkins did his research and recognized that Marriott had reinvented itself.

Becoming a Partner with Management

Equating buying a stock to becoming a partner with management, Hawkins generally won't buy a stock unless he has met with top executives of the company. He buys firms run by executives who own a substantial amount of stock in their companies, which tends to make them think and act like owners and run their businesses more efficiently. The number of shares executives own in a company can be found in a firm's proxy statement.

In the 1999 semiannual report to shareholders of his mutual funds, Hawkins discussed the rationale for his purchase of Seagram Company. Selling at $28 a share, Seagram was out of favor with investors when Hawkins decided to buy. He believed in the ability of CEO Edgar Bronfman Jr., based on his past track record, and recognized that the stock was undervalued. Hawkins knew that Bronfman's family owned 30 percent of Seagram. During the time Hawkins held the stock, Bronfman bought Universal Entertainment Group and sold Tropicana and USA Networks, which Hawkins says improved the value of the firm. Subsequently, prices climbed to between $50 and $65 and Hawkins sold.

Advice for Buying Mutual Funds

Speaking at an annual meeting, held for his mutual fund investors, Hawkins shared general advice for buying funds:

- Study the long-term performance record.
- Determine whether the manager and support team that built the performance record are still in place.
- Analyze the portfolio turnover record and after-tax returns.
- Understand the method and philosophy of the managers.
- Determine if the managers are investing their own money in the fund.

When buying mutual funds, read the prospectus, the statement of additional information, and the annual, semiannual, and quarterly reports, which can be requested from the fund. Look at the objective of the fund, the type of stocks or bonds held by the fund, and its long-term performance record. Both Morningstar and Value Line provide information about mutual funds.

Chapter 11

Applying Graham's Strategies for Different Types of Investors

BASED ON GRAHAM'S philosophy, conservative investors who purchase individual stocks would own a diversified portfolio of at least ten high-quality large firms, such as those in the S&P's 500 Index, with strong balance sheets and long-term records of consistent, growing earnings and dividends. Of course, stocks should be researched at the time of purchase to determine if the P/E and other criteria justify the purchase. Additionally, conservative investors would buy quality bonds—government bonds, corporate bonds, or municipal bonds, depending on their tax bracket. The top four ratings of Moody's and Standard & Poor's for corporate bonds, as shown in the next table, are considered investment grade. Bonds with lower ratings, referred to as junk bonds, can be bought with higher yields, paying higher interest income, but they are more speculative. Conservative investors would own few, if any, individual junk bonds, but might own some through mutual funds.

Bond Ratings

	Standard & Poor's	Moody's
AAA	Highest quality	Aaa
AA	High quality	Aa
A	High medium grade	Aa
BBB	Medium grade	Baa
Bb	Somewhat speculative	Ba
Ccc-C	Very speculative	Caa-C
D	In default	

A technique often used by bond buyers, called laddering maturities, involves diversifying by owning bonds with different maturities (coming due at different times). Short-term bonds mature in less than five years; intermediate bonds, five to ten years; and long-term bonds, more than ten years.

Graham suggested that investors hold at least 25 percent of their portfolios in bonds with an average seven- or eight-year maturity. The amount of money allocated to stocks versus bonds depends on an individual investor's income needs, investment risk tolerance, and current interest rates, as well as market conditions (for more about bond investing, see Chapter 21). Conservative investors also may choose to have their portfolios managed by a private money manager or to own mutual funds that include:

- Domestic stock mutual funds
- Global (domestic and foreign stocks) or international stock mutual funds
- U.S. government, corporate, and municipal bond funds
- Index funds (funds that mimic an index such as the S&P 500)

Moderate or aggressive investors have a wider range of investment options. They might own the same types of investments as conservative investors but also could add international stocks or domestic stocks of small and medium-size firms. These investors might purchase quality growth stocks and both investment grade and high-yielding bonds.

Chapter 12

The Life and Career of Benjamin Graham

GRAHAM WAS BORN in London in 1894 and, a year later, his family moved to New York. When he was nine, his father passed away, leaving his mother Dora with three young boys to raise. She tried to earn money in several business ventures but was unsuccessful. During his high school and college years, Graham took jobs to help support the family. In 1907, at age 13, he learned about the dangers of the stock market when his mother bought a few shares of U.S. Steel on margin, borrowing part of the money from her broker. The Federal Reserve System was not established until 1913, and bankers were the primary stabilizing force of the money supply. The most notable, John Pierpont Morgan, created an immense financial empire. After Dora made her stock purchase there was a run on the banks and the market plummeted. Morgan, along with other bankers, took action to restore confidence in the banking system and Wall Street with an infusion of money, but it was too late to save many small investors like Dora.

After completing high school, Graham was awarded a scholarship to Columbia. He excelled in math, English, and philosophy and, upon finishing his college education, received offers to teach each of these subjects at Columbia. Instead Graham went to work on Wall Street. Due to his nature and academic brilliance, Graham might have been happier at Columbia, but he was realistic about his need for money to help his family and himself. Although Graham took the more lucrative path the financial world offered, he later returned to his alma mater to teach. Professor Graham's security analysis classes were among the most successful and popular in the history of Columbia's business school.[1]

Shortly before World War I, Graham went to work in the bond department of a brokerage firm. After war broke out, in July 1914, investors frantically sold their stocks; to stop the panic, foreign exchanges were closed. Exchanges in Vienna, Berlin, Rome, Paris, London, and others shut down. To avoid a collapse, on July 31, 1914, the governing committee of the New York Stock Exchange (NYSE) voted to suspend trading. The NYSE opened again in mid-December, but restrictions were placed on prices and the trading of some stocks. These restraints were not lifted until 1915. This is the only time that the NYSE was closed for so long.[2]

When trading resumed, Graham's firm was understaffed and he worked at various jobs. As a result, he gained an understanding of how a Wall Street firm functioned, which was helpful to him later when he started his own business. He also became aware of the limited knowledge of many investors.

Graham Goes into Business and the Stock Market Crash of 1929–1932

During this time, stocks were bought on tips, rumors, and outright manipulation. Stock market operators raised large sums of money and purchased large blocks of stocks. After they bought stocks, operators circulated unfounded rumors such as pending earnings or dividend increases.[3] Once the price of a stock rose high enough, they sold. This was legal prior to the establishment of the Securities and Exchange Commission, which began operating in 1934.

Graham started his own investment firm in 1926, and Jerome Newman, an accountant, became his partner. In 1928, Graham began teaching evening courses in security analysis at his alma mater, Columbia, for the School of Business Administration. Graham-Newman was successful until the 1929 crash and the bear market that followed.[4]

From the high point of the market in 1929 to the low in 1932, the Dow Jones Industrial Average sank 89 percent. Prior to this, between 1925 and 1929, speculation had been rampant. Investors would buy stocks, putting up 10 percent to 25 percent of the price of a stock and borrowing the rest from their brokers (buying on margin).

The value of all the stocks listed on the NYSE in 1925 was $25 billion. By 1929, it was more than triple, almost $90 billion. Despite some warnings about an impending market correction and a weakening economy, the irrational optimism continued. Many investors bought into the euphoria and thought the market could only go one way—up. When the crash began on October 29, investors who bought on margin received calls from their brokers asking for more money (to cover their margin accounts) and they had to sell stocks to cover their losses. This and other factors contributed to heavy selling. By 1932, the market value of the stocks on the NYSE dropped from the 1929 high of $90 billion to less than $16 billion.[5]

Although Graham-Newman suffered financial losses and lost clients, the business still managed to survive while other Wall Street firms folded. In June 1932, writing for *Forbes* magazine, Graham pointed out that investors were ignoring stocks selling at bargain prices. He became bullish on the stock market before many of his colleagues. Examples of how drastically stocks had fallen include General Electric, which dropped from $400 a share in 1929 to $13 in 1932 and U.S. Steel, which fell from $262 in 1929 to $21 in 1932.[6] Toward the end of 1932, the market began its recovery. In the years that followed, Graham-Newman added new clients and the firm became successful again.

Drawing on his teachings from classes at Columbia, Graham and his coauthor, professor David Dodd, wrote *Security Analysis* in 1934 (McGraw-Hill). In 1949, Graham wrote *The Intelligent Investor* (HarperCollins). Both books have been updated and are considered investment classics.

A Lasting Legacy

After retiring in 1956, Graham moved to California and, subsequently, became a professor at UCLA's Graduate School of Business. He died September 21, 1976, at the age of 82.

Graham helped to raise the level of professionalism among security analysts and was instrumental in creating the professional designation of Chartered Financial Analyst (CFA). A special luncheon was held by the New York Society of Security Analysts in 1994 to honor him on the hundredth anniversary of his birth. Graham had been one of its founders and prominent members of the financial industry attended. Author Janet Lowe, who has written several books about Graham, equated his impact on investing to Babe Ruth's impact on baseball: both became role models that others could follow and build on. Former students of Graham's, Warren Buffett and other money managers, Walter Schloss and Irving Kahn, talked about how Graham had helped them start their careers.

Buffett gave a particularly eloquent speech describing his feelings and thoughts about Graham. He quoted Oscar Hammerstein, "A bell is not a bell 'til you ring it, a song is not a song 'til you sing it, and love in the heart isn't put there to stay, love isn't love 'til you give it away." Buffett said that Graham was like that about ideas—he shared his investment ideas with others, even when it put him at a competitive disadvantage. According to his former students, in his personal life, Graham was a charitable, caring person as well. Graham has truly left the investment world a legacy of lasting value.[7]

Phil Fisher:
The Investigative
Growth Stock
Investor

Unit Three
The Investigative
Growth Stock
Investor

P hil Fisher made millions for his clients and himself with his investigative process for finding highly profitable stocks. The Sherlock Holmes of investing, Fisher solves the mystery of whether a stock is worth buying by using the same talents as the famous fictitious detective: the power of observation, artful questioning, and logical deduction.

After completing preliminary research in his no-frills office, Fisher conducts a thorough investigation. He searches for growing companies with excellent management and products, a strong competitive edge, and tremendous profit potential. Fisher says: "I look for the really great growth stocks to hold for the long term—the only kind worth buying."

A pioneer of growth stock investing, Fisher has a following among investment professionals and individual investors. Fisher received national recognition when he wrote *Common Stocks and Uncommon Profits and Other Writings,* first published in 1958 and released again in 1997, incorporated with other previous writings by Fisher. After reading Fisher's original book, Warren Buffett was so impressed he traveled to California to meet Fisher and learn his strategies firsthand.

Fisher says that when he was about age 12 or 13, he learned about the stock market. He considered the stock market an exciting game offering him an opportunity to choose people and businesses that could be successful and at the same time make a lot of money. Now a master of this game, Fisher has developed his talent for judging corporate executives and the profit potential of their firms. To an extent, this skill is innate, but investors also can develop judgment skills as they gain investment experience.

While attending graduate school at Stanford University, Fisher studied with a management consultant who believed in a practical education. Every Wednesday, this professor would take the class to visit local firms and interview their top executives, asking questions about how they ran their businesses. Fisher learned how to question executives and the importance of a coordinated effort between all the divisions of a company.

In 1931, after working as a securities analyst, Fisher started his own business as a money manager and developed a comprehensive process for evaluating companies. One of his first winning stock purchases was a company called Food Machinery, now known as FMC. Just a few years before, he had watched his professor interview the executives of two firms, which merged and became part of FMC. According to Fisher, he sold this stock at a gain of 50 times his original purchase price. He has since bought stocks of other successful firms. Among them are Motorola, Texas Instruments, Dow Chemical, and Raychem (Raychem was acquired by Tyco International in 1999).[1]

Chapter 13

Fisher's Success Strategies: Evaluating a Company's People, Products, and Policies

EARLY IN HIS career, Fisher had both a long-term and short-term strategy for buying and selling stocks. He found his profits were substantially lower and his life a lot more stressful when he bought and sold stocks for short-term profits. As a result, Fisher decided to buy only stocks of companies that he believed had outstanding long-term growth potential. "Of course," he cautions, "if you try to buy the really great growth stock, you may decide you made a mistake, or after following and getting to know the company, determine you shouldn't have bought it. In either case, you should sell the shares whether you have a profit or a loss. What is important is that if you have a loss, it is small compared to the big gains that just one really outstanding stock can produce when you hold it for the long term."[1]

Fisher pays more attention to the quality of people, products, and policies of firms than to their past financial numbers. After reading financial reports, he gathers background information about his purchase candidate. He speaks by phone or in person with customers, suppliers, competitors, and others knowledgeable about the company. Then, if the company is worthy of further consideration, he meets with the firm's top executives and questions them about their businesses.

Fisher's son Ken, a well-known money manager and *Forbes* columnist; Warren Buffett; and other investors have modified Fisher's process to meet their investment needs and combined his criteria with their own.

Today, there is an enormous amount of information available to investors through the Internet and computer databases. Generally, corporate executives are more responsive and accessible to shareholders or prospective shareholders.

Chapter 14

Fisher Applies the 3 Steps: Getting the Scuttlebutt

Step 1: Gather the Information

Fisher reads publications like *Forbes, Fortune, Barron's,* and *The Wall Street Journal* but gets his investment leads primarily through talking with investment professionals and businesspeople. He studies company reports and stock research reports.

Investors can obtain company reports by calling a firm's investor relations department or visiting a company's Web site. Names of a company's key customers, competitors, and suppliers may be determined through research or provided by the investor relations department.

Standard & Poor's Industry Surveys lists industry publications. The Gale Group (www.galegroup.com) sells databases such as Infotrac, available in many libraries and universities, which can be used to research companies and the executives who run them. These databases contain summaries of current and past articles from business magazines, newspapers, industry trade journals, and investment reports. The Gale Group also publishes *The Encyclopedia of Emerging Industries.* Additionally, Hoover's offers company profiles in print, on CD-ROM, and online at (hoovers.com).

Step 2: Evaluate the Information

To decide if a firm meets his criteria, Fisher asks questions such as:

- Does the company have an outstanding CEO and a strong management team?
- Are the executives candid in reporting problems as well as favorable business news to shareholders?
- Do the executives have a track record of innovative policies and products?
- Does the company have a long-term commitment to producing high-quality products of significant value to customers?
- Does the firm maintain excellent customer and employee relations?
- Does the company have a competitive edge and the ability to cope with change?
- Is the business efficiently run with favorable, sustainable profit margins and increasing sales and earnings?
- Is the stock selling at a reasonable price relative to the long-term potential of earnings and future stock price?

Using Measures That Matter

In 1997, a study funded by Ernst & Young called "Measures That Matter" was conducted by Professor Sarah Mavrinac and Tony Siesfeld. This study included nonfinancial performance measures that analysts consider to determine the value of a company. Fisher has applied many of these measures:

- (Successful) Execution of corporate strategy
- Management credibility and experience
- Accessibility of management
- Innovation
- Ability to attract and retain talented people
- Customer-perceived quality of products
- Customer satisfaction
- Brand image
- Product durability
- New product development cycle time and efficiency
- Strength of marketing and advertising

The Importance of Innovative Executives

Fisher seeks companies run by innovative executives with a history of successful achievements. This is especially important in an industry he has favored, technology, because products become obsolete quickly and competition is fierce. Business risks of technology firms, which are discussed in cautionary statements of company reports, also include expiration of patents and potential difficulties in developing, producing, testing, marketing, and selling products. These firms also may have difficulty attracting and retaining key technical marketing and management staff because experienced people in the technology field have been in high demand.

Innovation is often associated with producing unique, quality products or services perceived by customers to be of higher value than the competitors' products. But innovation can apply to any aspect of a business: organizational structure, use of new technologies to improve productivity, policies related to customer service, employee benefits or training, and joint ventures. Capable, innovative corporate executives are disciplined in their financial controls and in setting objectives but are flexible in other ways such as refocusing their direction or changing policies when necessary.

Texas Instruments, a firm that has been one of Fisher's holdings, is an example. The company was founded in 1930 as Geophysical Service, specializing in the reflection seismograph method of exploration. In 1938, Erik Jonsson, a bright engineer, became president and led the company in a new direction. Under Jonsson's leadership, Texas Instruments applied new technology and created the first U.S. Navy submarine-detection equipment during World War II.

In 1952, Texas Instruments began making transistors and entered the semiconductor business. Subsequently, the company designed the first commercial transistor radio, Regency. The success of this radio helped Texas Instruments become an important supplier of components to IBM for its computers and to other firms.

In 1956, Fisher was introduced to Jonsson by a mutual acquaintance. After researching the company, he was impressed enough to buy Texas Instruments stock for his clients and himself, making it a major holding. In 1967, Jonsson retired, Mark Shepherd became president, and the company invented the electronic hand-held calculator.

In 1978, Shepherd became chairman, and the company introduced Speak & Spell, a product that synthesized speech. Shepherd created programs encouraging employee contributions to the business and he stressed the importance of employee relations, a policy still carried out by the firm. Today, Texas Instruments employee profit sharing is directly tied to operating profit margins based on how the company performs. This ties every employee directly to building shareholder value.

In 1996, Texas Instruments executives once again decided to refocus and concentrate on digital signal processing (DSPs). Speaking at the 1999 annual meeting, current chairman Tom Engibous talked about the various applications of DSPs. He explained that the firm's DSPs power digital cell phones and are found in medical equipment (MRIs and digital hearing aids), entertainment products (digital speakers), cameras, and televisions. One of the hottest gifts for Christmas 1998 was a toy called Furby, a talking animal powered by Texas Instruments' digital technology. A vision Engibous holds is that someday the firm's DSPs "will be the key to creating artificial limbs that simulate the sense of touch and also provide tools that could let blind people see."

Engibous also talked about the difficult work it took to become the leader in DSPs, saying that the company had to go through 14 divestitures, 10 acquisitions, and a major restructuring from 1996 to 1999. Investors were impressed by the company's commitment, and, as a result, the stock price increased more than 300 percent.

Fisher bought Texas Instruments stock at $14 a share.[1] By the third quarter of 1999, after several stock splits, each share Fisher bought became 1,749.6 shares (according to Texas Instruments' calculations) and the stock sold for about $93. This means each share purchased in 1956 at $14 grew to $162,712.[2]

Fisher's View of Financial Numbers and Ratios

Fisher begins his research by studying a company's reports. Reading the CEO's letter and management's discussion in annual reports, he analyzes performance numbers, research and development (R&D) activities, goals, and business risks. By evaluating the assets and liabilities shown on the firm's balance sheet, he looks for firms with low debt and good financial strength. He studies the income statement, comparing current sales and earnings as well as costs and expenses with those of previous years. Fisher pays attention to the notes of the firm's financial statements and evaluates information about extraordinary earnings or expenses, changes in accounting, or other disclosures.

He reads the proxy statement, which lists salaries, stock ownership, and stock options held by the top executives and directors. If the top executives own a substantial amount of shares, their interests tend to be more aligned with shareholders. The proxy statement includes a graph comparing a company's stock performance with a stock market index, such as the S&P 500 Index, and with a sector or subgroup(s) of industry peers within the index. The term *sector* refers to companies that are in similar businesses. Performance numbers can also be illustrated in dollar amounts. The 1999 proxy statement of Texas Instruments, for example, showed that an initial investment of $100 in Texas Instruments stock from 1993 to 1998 grew to $565 (with all dividends reinvested). During the same period, $100 invested in the S&P 500 Index would have grown to $294 and, in the S&P Technology Sector Index, $514.

The S&P technology sector consists of companies in the fields of computers, electronics, communications equipment, and photography/imaging, such as Lucent Technologies, Motorola, Microsoft, Novell, International Business Machines (IBM), Intel, Oracle, Cisco Systems, and National Semiconductor.

Fisher evaluates some financial numbers and ratios, such as R&D expenditures and profit margins, but his emphasis is on how the numbers were created and he wants to know what the company is doing to produce substantial future profits.

Learn What the Company Is Doing to Maintain Profit Margins

It's not enough for Fisher to know that a company has favorable profit margins—he also questions how management plans to maintain profit margins. The profit margin, an indicator of how efficiently management is running a company, shows the amount of sales being turned into earnings. In order to achieve strong profit margins, a firm should be increasing sales while keeping costs and expenses low, resulting in higher profits.

Fisher evaluates the operating profit margin: operating earnings (earnings from the main business as opposed to earnings from other sources such as income from investments) before interest, depreciation, and taxes, divided by sales, and expressed as a percentage (as discussed in Chapter 3). The operating profit margin is compared with previous years' margins to determine the trend, and with competitors' profit margins.

There are various reasons profit margins may be higher or lower. One of Fisher's holdings, Motorola, in the semiconductor and cellular communications business, had a low profit margin in 1998, in part due to the global economic problems. Subsequently, the economic recovery of foreign countries where Motorola sells products as well as restructuring and other internal changes within the business helped increase profit margins. Motorola's operating profit margin for 1999 was 14.5 percent, compared to its 1998 operating margin of 10.3 percent.

A method that Motorola developed in the late 1980s, which helped create higher profit margins, was to reduce cycle time. This is the time from receipt of orders to delivery and from development of products to shipment. Reducing cycle time by establishing a faster, more efficient process creates faster inventory turnover, lowers costs, and helps increase profit margins. In the 1990s, the effective use of computer software programs has increased efficiency of scheduling, billing, and inventory control for businesses. Restructuring, successful joint ventures, and intelligent use of the Internet to do business have helped increase profit margins. Information about policies or technologies used to create profit margins may be found by reading company reports. Investors also may question executives or representatives of investor relations departments to determine what a company is doing to improve or maintain profit margins.

Profit margins change from year to year and can vary among industries and within sectors.

Operating Profit Margins (Year-to-Year Comparisons for the Technology Sector)

	1995	1996	1997	1998
Electronics	11.1	10.3	10.4	9.5
Semiconductors	25.9	25.7	28.0	24.1
Computer and Peripheral	16.2	13.7	14.6	12.7
Computer Software and Services	27.3	27.2	29.3	31.5

Source: *Value Line Investment Survey*

Paying Dividends or Reinvesting Earnings

Growth companies typically pay low or no cash dividends. Texas Instruments and Motorola, for example, paid about 20 percent of earnings in dividends on average for the five years ending 1998. Microsoft paid no dividend, and Intel paid a dividend of about 4 percent of earnings.

Dividends are not important to Fisher. He is primarily concerned with whether retained earnings are being invested wisely to produce future earnings growth. Growing companies can use money otherwise paid out in dividends more effectively to pay for R&D, new technologies, and advertising and marketing in anticipation of creating higher earnings.

Evaluating the P/E and P/S

Although he may look at the price-to-earnings (P/E) ratio of a stock, Fisher believes investors put too much emphasis on this ratio. When he buys a stock he wants to feel reasonably confident the firm will have much higher earnings growth over the long term, resulting in much higher stock prices. To Fisher, what's important is the current stock price in relation to the company's long-term future potential earnings.

Fisher also may look at the price-to-sales ratio (P/S), but like the P/E, this ratio would not have a great deal of significance for him. Nevertheless, many investors use the P/S and it is helpful to understand how it can be applied. Fisher's son Ken was a pioneer in bringing the P/S to the investment world.

Even well-established companies have problems from time to time, especially in the technology field, and some firms may report very low earnings or losses. In this case, because the company has a high P/E or no P/E, investors may evaluate the stock based on the P/S instead of the P/E (the P/S may also be used as an additional measure in other circumstances). To calculate the P/S ratio, divide the stock's price by the company's sales per share.

Motorola, for instance, was selling at a low of about $38 in 1998, down from its high of $66 and its 1997 high of $90. Motorola sells products worldwide and its earnings suffered because of the severe economic problems in Asia and other parts of the world. Additionally, management was slow in changing from analog to digital cellular equipment, already accomplished by competitors. Motorola reported earnings per share of $.58 (a P/E of 66) and sales per share of $48 (a P/S of under 1). A P/S ratio of 3 is considered reasonable, 1 or less very attractive, but this varies from industry to industry, and like other ratios, should be compared to industry competitors. Motorola refocused, restructured, cut costs, produced new products, and at the end of 1999 the stock was $147 (as of June 1, 2000, Motorola had a three-for-one stock split).

"Getting the Scuttlebutt"

Aware that investing is an art, not a science, Fisher tries to get as complete a picture of his purchase candidates as possible. Going beyond company reports, Fisher seeks out firsthand information from people related to the company, which he refers to as "getting the scuttlebutt." This process is known by investment professionals as the mosaic concept, because it is thought of as putting together the various pieces of background information describing a firm. To get background information in a similar manner to Fisher's, investment professionals following the mosaic concept attempt to contact people by phone or in person related to or knowledgeable about their purchase candidates. Somewhat like getting references, obtaining this information may include speaking with:

- Customers
- Suppliers or other vendors who deal with the firm
- Executives of competing companies
- Buyers or salespeople of stores that sell the firm's products
- Securities analysts who follow the company
- Competitors

- Consultants who work with the firm or who are familiar with the business
- Creditors of the firm
- Technicians and industry experts
- Others related to the company

Fisher may gain insight into a company as these people share their perceptions of how the business operates and the caliber of management. He seeks answers to questions such as: What do customers think about the quality of products and service? What do executives of competing firms think of the company? How does the company compare with other companies in the industry?

Talking with suppliers may provide information to help determine the current business condition of a company and its industry. Suppliers or other vendors and technicians in the field might share knowledge about technologies related to the industry.

Some investment professionals who follow the mosaic concept may speak with employees to find out about employee relations and other aspects of a business. This is a sensitive area, because companies can restrict what employees say about the business, but while getting background data, investors will often discover information about employee relations.

In addition to employee relations, the way executives work together is important. Turnover of key executives may be an indicator of problems. Information about key executives can be found in newspaper and magazine articles about companies, and the names of key executives are listed in company reports.

From background information he has gathered, Fisher evaluates the strength of the management team. "If there is a clash between division heads, a them-versus-us attitude, or an ego problem between the CEO and other executives, an otherwise successful company may fall apart," Fisher says. A CEO with an unhealthy ego, who wants to take credit for achievements instead of developing and supporting those under him or her, creates a problem that may show up in a loss of valuable employees and ultimately in reduced profits.

If Fisher can't gain access to enough people or obtain enough information, he will stop his research and find another purchase candidate.

Fisher Meets with the Top Executives

After completing his background research and armed with the information, Fisher sets out to meet with top executives of the company. By this time, he has a good understanding of the business and can ask germane questions.

Fisher's questions might relate to items on the firm's financial statements, new technologies, R&D activities, advertising and marketing, cost controls and expenses, or competitive problems. Fisher says that because each business is different, his questions vary with the type of business and what he has learned from his research. Some general questions he might ask the executives are:

- What long-term business problems does your company face and how do you plan to handle them?
- What are your future plans for R&D?
- What actions are being taken to overcome (current, specific) business problems?
- How will changes in consumer buying affect your firm?
- How will your international operations be affected by business trends and economic conditions of countries where you do business?

It takes time to get to know management, and sometimes after Fisher purchases a stock and holds it for a while, he discovers new facts that change his opinion. Evaluating management is an ongoing process and continues after a stock has been bought.

Step 3: Make the Decision

Before buying a stock, Fisher makes sure he has enough information, his questions have been answered sufficiently, and the firm meets his criteria. To review questions Fisher would ask regarding his criteria, see page 96 at the beginning of this chapter. Chapter 15, Motorola Revisited, gives further insight into how Fisher applies his criteria.

Fisher only buys a stock if he believes the company has outstanding long-term profit potential based on his overall assessment of the firm. He evaluates the current price in relation to future potential earnings and stock price. Fisher has bought stocks before other investors have recognized the company's value or even when many investors were negative about the company. What matters to Fisher is not that others agree with him, but that he has done thorough research and feels confident about making the investment. He prefers to buy stocks during general market declines or at times when a stock is dropping due to a bad quarter or the news of business problems he believes are temporary.

To monitor his holdings, Fisher reads company reports and stock research reports, and he makes follow-up visits or phone calls when appropriate. If there is news of business problems, Fisher may do further research and call the company to find out what management is doing to correct the situation. Fisher sells when the firm no longer meets his buying criteria or if he finds his original assessment was incorrect.

Chapter 15

Motorola Revisited

MOTOROLA HAS BEEN an outstanding company and a profitable stock for Fisher. He made his first purchase of Motorola in 1956, but he actually learned about the company during World War II when he served in the U.S. Army Airforce (the Air Force became a separate division of the Armed Forces in 1947) and later on the Surplus Board. He knew that the military thought very highly of Motorola's products. At that time, the company was called Galvin Manufacturing.

More than a decade later, after speaking with an analyst about Motorola, Fisher researched the company and traveled to its headquarters in Illinois by special arrangement. He spent hours with Motorola's top officers—Paul Galvin, CEO and founder; his son Bob, president; and Matt Hickey, vice president of finance.

Fisher recalled: "I was very impressed with what I saw, particularly with the potential I believed I saw in Bob Galvin from the first time I met him. One of the things I noticed was the manner in which Galvin expressed himself. Galvin would often use the exact word that precisely and accurately fit the meaning he desired to convey. Although there may not be a perfect correlation, it has been my experience that people who express themselves precisely are apt to be clear thinkers in their ideas. Those who talk in generalities and sloppy terms are apt to be somewhat sloppy in their actions."

Soon after Fisher purchased Motorola stock for his clients and himself, he found out that some Wall Street analysts had a negative opinion of the company. They even criticized the fact that Bob Galvin was president, calling this an example of extreme nepotism. These analysts were wrong about the firm and about Bob Galvin. Because they didn't do their research, they missed a great buying opportunity.[1]

From the time he joined Motorola, Bob Galvin worked at various jobs in different departments—the inspection department, the packing line, and the laboratory, where he received intensive training in electronics. Paul Galvin tested his son through decisions made by Bob regarding the business. Bob earned the respect of company employees and has since been recognized worldwide as one of the great corporate leaders of our time.

Despite analysts' negative opinions, Fisher held Motorola for the long term. Fisher bought the stock for his clients and himself, paying between $42 and $43 a share. Most of his clients bought 1,000 or 2,000 shares, making the total cost for a 1,000-share block under $43,000. As of year-end 1997, each of those original purchases of $43,000 that were still intact (after adjusting for stock splits) had a market value of over $10 million. The brief history of Motorola that follows gives details of how Fisher applied his criteria to this company. This criteria can be applied to other businesses as well.[2]

Criteria: An Innovative, Capable CEO

Paul Galvin (1895–1959) began the operations of Galvin Manufacturing in 1928. The firm's name was changed to Motorola in 1947. Galvin was considered by those who knew him to be a hardworking, straight-talking man of high integrity. He started the business with $565 in cash, $750 in tools, and a design for a device called the battery eliminator. The eliminator, used exclusively with radios, became obsolete soon after the company began operations because new radios that plugged directly into the AC current came onto the market. To solve the problem of how to stay in business, Galvin developed another product, the first commercial car radio. Marketed under the trade name Motorola, it became known as America's finest car radio.

Criteria Applied: *Paul Galvin was the type of CEO Fisher seeks. Galvin was candid, capable, and innovative. He created the car radio,* *rescuing Motorola from bankruptcy, and under his leadership the firm developed other outstanding products.*

Criteria: Excellent Employee Relations

In the early days of Motorola, employee benefits and government regulations, as we know them today, didn't exist. Paul Galvin felt that employees should be treated with respect and dignity. His concern for employees extended beyond the day-to-day business of the company. He helped them in various ways: assisting employees and their family members who were ill to get medical care; paying for the childbirth expenses of employees and spouses; funding college tuition for employees' children when they couldn't afford it. After the business was more successful, bonuses were paid. Motorola was one of the first firms in the United States to establish a profit-sharing plan. Policies also were instituted to reward employees financially for ideas they contributed that benefitted the firm. Recognized for excellent employee relations, Motorola has been listed in *The 100 Best Companies to Work for in America,* a book by Robert Levering and Milton Moskowitz (currently available as a series of articles for *Fortune* magazine). The company also has been listed among *Fortune*'s "America's Most Admired Corporations." Unfortunately, due to business conditions brought on in part by the economic global problems that began in 1997, Motorola had to restructure, close plants, and reduce the number of its employees. Much of this was done through retirements and sales of businesses.

Criteria Applied: *If a company's employee relations are poor, it can show up in lower productivity, lower profits, and a lower stock price. Fisher considers employee relations an important aspect of his overall evaluation of a company. Motorola has had excellent employee relations*

Criteria: A Firm Committed to Consistently Producing Products of Significant Value to Consumers

Motorola has had a long-term commitment to R&D. The firm's products include semiconductors, cellular phones and other wireless global communications systems, pagers, and two-way radio systems. The company has a history of innovative products and policies. Paul

Galvin made a major contribution during World War II by creating effective communications for the United States and its allies. The Handie-Talkie two-way radio developed by Motorola was used by all branches of the U.S. armed services. In the infantry, this piece of equipment was second only to the rifle in importance. Later, Dan Noble, an engineer hired by Galvin, developed a longer-range communications device that earned Army-Navy awards. After the war, Noble set up an R&D facility, which helped Motorola become one of the world's largest manufacturers of semiconductors.

Criteria Applied: *Fisher looks for companies with outstanding products. Having researched Motorola, he was aware of its high-quality products.*

Criteria: Outstanding Business Leadership

Bob Galvin established the Motorola training and education center, called Motorola University, during a time when some corporate executives didn't think employee training was important. One program, the Manager of Managers, taught by the company's top executives, covers past business successes and failures and helps employees find their own strengths and weaknesses. This ultimately translates into financial benefits. Motorola University gives the company an opportunity to find and promote future leaders from within the business. Bob Galvin also built on his father's policy of decentralized management, which means decisions can be made on the operating business level.

In 1988, under Bob Galvin's leadership, Motorola was awarded the first Malcolm Baldridge National Quality Award, given by Congress to encourage the pursuit of quality in American business. Galvin has received many other awards.

Criteria Applied: *Fisher's original assessment of Bob Galvin was confirmed by Galvin's innovative policies and ideas and the recognition he later received for outstanding leadership. Motorola University contributes to the development of future business leaders.*

Criteria: A Firm Capable of Coping with Competition and Change

Although Japan's stock market and economy experienced severe problems during the 1990s, in the mid-1980s, Japanese businesses were so strong they were a threat to American firms such as Motorola. U.S. firms were in serious danger of folding and some collapsed because of their inability to compete successfully with Japanese companies. While the Japanese may have had good products, they also had a one-sided competitive edge. Japanese businesses could sell their products in the United States almost without restriction, but the sale of U.S. products was restricted in Japan. In addition, the Japanese government worked closely with Japanese companies. Japanese leaders targeted businesses they wanted to dominate and assisted their own companies by funding research for products. They also helped their businesses determine prices that would undercut competition.

Motorola's semiconductor business was threatened because U.S. manufacturers making products requiring semiconductors such as computers and scientific instruments were placing orders with the Japanese. Semiconductors produced by the Japanese were of much higher value because they had a substantially lower percentages of defective units. During this time, Motorola was manufacturing televisions in competition with Japanese businesses.

Bob Galvin made some bold moves, leading the way for U.S. firms to combat the competition. Realizing that he could not compete with Japanese televisions, Galvin sold Motorola's television business to Matsushita Electric Industrial Company. He made an extensive study of Japanese management methods and used Japanese products as a benchmark. As a result, Motorola made dramatic improvements in reducing the percentage of defects in semiconductors as well as other products. The firm produced products of such high quality that Motorola gained a significant market share in Japan as well as in China.

Criteria Applied: *Fisher buys stocks of companies that not only have a competitive edge, but also the determination to keep up with competition and change, which Motorola demonstrated.*

Criteria: An Efficiently Run Business and Increasing Earnings

Bob Galvin had a goal of continually improving productivity and profitability. In Motorola's 1986 annual report, Galvin said: "We have concentrated our fixed asset expenditures on equipment that improves quality and enhances productivity."

Galvin and his management team developed innovative approaches. One was reducing cycle time, an important method of lowering expenses and controlling costs. Shorter manufacturing cycles resulted in lower inventories and more efficient use of assets.

In Motorola's 1987 annual report, the concept was explained to shareholders: "Cycle time starts from the moment a customer places an order for an existing product to the time we deliver it. In the case of new products, it is the time span between when we conceive of the product until it ships. To reduce cycle time, we examine the total system, including design, marketing, and administration to determine how we can improve the process, and make it more efficient." Motorola greatly improved the total system and shortened cycle time. This concept has been widened to increase efficiency and cut costs throughout the company.

Motorola's executives have been committed to long-term growth and the company has shown substantial increases in earnings and sales. Sales increased from $3.284 billion in 1980 to $29.794 billion in 1997; earnings went from $192 million in 1980 to $1.180 billion in 1997. This translated into shareholder profits as Motorola's stock price climbed from a low of $6 a share in 1980 to a high of more than $90 in 1997.

Criteria Applied: *Fisher estimates potential growth of a company's earnings based on his complete analysis of the business. Motorola's stock performance and past sales and earnings reflect Fisher's initial evaluation and continuous monitoring of this company as an outstanding long-term investment.*

In 1997, Bob Galvin's son, Chris, took over as CEO of Motorola, after having worked for the company for many years. Once again, like his father and grandfather, Chris Galvin was at the helm when the company faced serious problems. In 1998, sales and earnings declined. Demand for pagers fell off in China, and Motorola's inventories increased. As global semiconductor business declined, competitors cut into the sales of cellular telephones and handsets.

Galvin and his management team took action. Plants were sold, divisions reorganized, and other changes were implemented. Motorola announced new products and increased investment in R&D with a goal of strengthening technology leadership and long-term growth of sales and earnings. In 1999, the firm began to recover. The stock had been as low as $38 a share in 1998 and by the end of 1999 was $147. Fisher used sound judgment in investigating and selecting Motorola. He had the courage of his convictions to hold the stock despite adverse opinions from Wall Street, stayed with it when others might have sold because of fear or greed, and he and his clients were rewarded.

Chapter 16

Applying Fisher's Strategies for Different Investment Types

ALTHOUGH FISHER'S CRITERIA can be applied to most types of businesses and for all types of investors, his scuttlebutt approach is most applicable for enterprising moderate or aggressive investors. Investors researching smaller, local or nearby regional companies may have greater ability to contact customers, suppliers, competitors, or others related to the company, as Fisher does. Often, there is more local media coverage of local or regional firms. Attending industry conventions and trade shows where the firm's products are displayed may also give investors a chance to talk with employees as well as competitors.

Whether an investor is successful in applying Fisher's scuttlebutt process depends on his or her access to people knowledgeable about the company and to the firm's top executives. Success is also dependent on the investor's ability to discreetly acquire and competently apply the information gained from this research.

Question the Executives about Their Companies

Professional investors like Fisher have access to top executives generally not available to most individual investors. But enterprising investors have been able to speak with executives by phone or in person. For example, Andrew Walker, a student from Virginia, studied company reports, and spoke with editors of investment newsletters (covering his purchase candidates) and others. After completing his background research, Andrew called the company and asked intelligent questions about specific areas such as debt obligations and current operations. He spoke with CFOs and CEOs. Mary Beck, a grandmother from Florida, along with members of an investment club she had joined, arranged visits to companies in advance and met with top executives. Some corporate executives speak at regional or national conferences of the National Association of Investors Corporation (investment clubs) and will answer investors' questions. Investment club members as a group or investors who own a substantial number of shares of a firm may have better access to upper management.

If it is not possible to speak with management, questions may be answered by knowledgeable representatives of investor relations departments. The level of expertise of representatives in investor relations departments varies from company to company, and it may be best to speak with the department head. Prior to speaking with corporate executives or contacting the investor relations departments, have a thorough understanding of the business and a list of well-thought-out questions.

Other Sources of Background Information

Investors who lack time or ability to emulate Fisher's process and more passive, conservative investors may get background information from the following alternative sources.

Company Conference Calls

Participants of company conference calls conducted by a firm's top executives include analysts, investors, and media members. Louis M. Thompson Jr., president and CEO of the National Investor Relations Institute, describes the calls: "During conference calls, corporate executives discuss quarterly earnings reports and other important announcements about the firm, which have been released to the press a short time before the call. Typically, the CFO or president answers questions from analysts who follow the firm. Companies set up conference calls with special phone numbers and investors can call in and listen or participate, depending on the firm's policy. Firms may record the calls, provide a phone number for the replay, and also may place a transcript or recording of the call or broadcast the call in real time on the company's Web site."[1] Best Calls (bestcalls.com) lists upcoming conference calls and offers e-mail reminders of conference calls. Participating or listening to these calls may be of help, along with other information, in evaluating the management of a firm.

Company Web Sites

Although company Web sites are self-serving, analysts use them as a source of information and nonprofessional investors can as well. Company Web sites provide financial reports, news releases, speeches of top executives, product information, a history of the firm, and additional information. Some companies send investors quarterly sales and earnings reports via e-mail. Other firms notify investors via e-mail of upcoming events like annual meetings and may place transcripts, recordings, and videos of annual meetings on their Web sites or broadcast the meetings in real time.

Learn about the Products and Get Competitors' Opinions of the Company

Many investors, including Warren Buffett, find out what customers think about products by becoming a customer, then buying a company whose products they already use and like. Of course, how practical this is depends on the type of products involved. When shopping for products, compare prices, quality, design, packaging, performance, and any special features with competitors' products and, at the same time, get opinions from people who sell the products. *Consumer Reports* and other product research services may also be good sources of information.

One way of finding out competitors' opinions is to contact executives or investor relations departments of several competing firms and ask how the competing firm compares to the stock purchase candidate.

Industry trade magazines and business publications may have articles that contain information about a firm's employee relations. This can be researched on the Internet or by using Infotrac. *Fortune* magazine's "100 Best Companies to Work For" lists firms that have good employee relations. In addition, investor relations departments as well as company reports often have information concerning the firm's policies for attracting and retaining employees, such as benefits and training.

Research the Top Executives

Reading past company reports, speeches, and interviews to find out what executives have said about their goals and their financial projections in comparison with the results may help evaluate their abilities. This information should be available from the investor relations department and through other research.

Background information about executives may be obtained from current and past articles in business publications, industry trade journals, and investment reports. This can be accomplished using Infotrac or visiting Web sites on the Internet. The Wall Street Journal Interactive Edition (wsj.com), Microsoft (msn.com), and Wall Street City (wallstreetcity.com) have links to other sites with archives of news articles (there may be a fee or subscription required).

Use Professional Management

Investors who want to employ a private money manager or to select a mutual fund can evaluate the performance track records for the past five or ten years and find out if the manager's investment process goes beyond financial numbers and ratios. Money managers who emulate Fisher's investment strategies would have a low portfolio turnover rate, generally holding stocks for the long term instead of buying and selling stocks for the short term. When selecting mutual funds, it is advisable to study the prospectus and the annual and quarterly reports.

Chapter 17

Thorns and Roses: Learning from Investment Mistakes

"INVESTMENT MISTAKES SHOULD be used as a learning experience," according to Fisher. "Investors should reflect on their mistakes—the thorns—rather than thinking or talking only about their winners— the roses. The focus is not on the fact that mistakes have been made, some are inevitable. What matters is that you can learn something from them."

Fisher says that he made mistakes purchasing three different stocks, with long intervals between each, because he did not follow his investigative process as closely as he usually does. Looking back on this, Fisher feels that had he investigated more thoroughly, he would have uncovered information to stop him from making these investments.

Misjudging the quality of management is another reason Fisher gives for mistakes. He explains: "The reason for my big successes is that management of the companies involved had unusual ingenuity, outstanding policies, and basic business ability. Sometimes executives appear to have these traits, but they do not have the ability to execute them. These factors can only be determined over time." This is the area in which some of Fisher's mistakes have occurred, even though the net loss has been very small. Although he has made errors in judgment, Fisher remarks, "I am grateful to the managers who spent time with me prior to and during the time I owned their stocks." The final reason he cites for his mistakes is due to deceit or concealment by management, which occurred in very few cases. Fisher says that his total losses have been insignificant in relation to the large gains made from stocks of companies he has held for many years.[1]

Chapter 18

The Life and Career
of Phil Fisher

FISHER WAS BORN September 8, 1907. He describes his father as a dedicated surgeon who cared more about humanity than becoming wealthy. Fisher's father often charged very low fees and the family was of moderate means. "When I was around age 12 or 13, I learned about the stock market," Fisher recalls. He viewed the stock market as a game that offered him an opportunity to choose people and companies that could be highly successful and to make a lot of money.

A bright student, Fisher enrolled in college when he was 15 and started graduate school at Stanford a few years later. One of his professors, Dr. Emmett, was a management consultant who taught a unique class in business management. "Instead of the normal classroom atmosphere, every Wednesday our class visited a different major plant in the Bay Area. We toured plants of companies and after the tour, as the students listened, Dr. Emmett questioned managers about their business policies and how they were conducting operations," Fisher says. From these classes, Fisher learned how to conduct interviews and recognize the basic components of a successful business: quality management, products, and marketing. During one of his class field trips, Fisher was impressed by the executives, products, and profit potential of two firms located near each other. This particular trip turned out to be of value to him when he later became a money manager.

After working as a security analyst, Fisher started his own business as a money manager in 1931, during the Great Depression. By 1933, he was still struggling to make a living. The stock market was at a low point, the Dow Jones Industrial Average had crashed 89 percent between 1929 and 1932, and investors were experiencing the worst bear market in U.S. history. One of the stocks that plummeted caught Fisher's attention. The two companies that impressed Fisher during Dr. Emmett's class visit had merged with a third and gone public. The stock of the resulting company, Food Machinery, now known as FMC, was selling at about $4 a share, off from a high of around $50. Fisher knew that FMC was well run and had outstanding products. He took advantage of this great buying opportunity, purchasing the stock for his clients and himself.

The economy pulled out of the Depression, the market turned around, and FMC became a big winner for Fisher. "I held the stock until it reached a point when I felt the company would not continue to have the type of growth it had in previous years. I sold my clients' stock and my own. My records show the gain was over 50 times the original investment," Fisher remarked. After this purchase, his business took off and his reputation as a money manager soared.[1]

Three Generations of Fishers

Fisher is very proud of his family. Two members have followed him into the investment field, his son Ken, a money manager, and his grandson Clay, who at age 16 wrote a book for young investors about the stock market. The author of three books, Ken is also known for his column "Portfolio Strategy" in *Forbes* magazine—the seventh-longest-running column in *Forbes*' 80-plus-year history.

Ken Fisher is founder, chairman, and CEO of Fisher Investments. His company manages money for Fortune 500 companies, foundations, endowments, and individual investors. Although he learned about investing from his father and applies some of Phil Fisher's strategies and criteria, Ken has his own distinctive investment style. A pioneer in the use of computers for screening stocks, Ken puts more emphasis on financial numbers and evaluates economic and technical statistics, the business outlook, the direction of interest rates, and general stock market indicators.[2]

At age 92, Phil Fisher believes it is important for seniors to keep active. He attributes his longevity to eating healthy foods and getting some form of exercise every day.[3] A modern-day hero, Fisher has made a great contribution to the field of growth investing.

PART IV

Thomas Rowe Price: The Visionary Growth Investor

Thomas Rowe Price, founder of T. Rowe Price Associates, the mutual fund and money management firm, made a fortune for his clients and himself investing in companies with high growth potential selling at reasonable prices. Using common sense and forward thinking, Price interpreted changes in economic, political, and social trends affecting businesses to help him make investment decisions.[1]

Like Jules Verne, the 19th-century author who could foresee trends and inventions such as television and space satellites, Price was considered a futurist in the investment field. *Forbes* magazine referred to him as "the sage of Baltimore." *Barron's* called his career the "triumph of a visionary."

George A. Roche, chairman and president of T. Rowe Price Associates says, "Price gave us fundamental principles of investing that our firm is still following today."[2] Price's timeless investment advice can be applied to current as well as future stock and bond markets.

In the 1930s, many investors were buying cyclical stocks—railroad and auto companies—but Price was purchasing growth stocks. Some of the stocks he bought then are still well known to investors, such as Coca-Cola, Dow Chemical, and Minnesota Mining (3M). After working for a brokerage firm, Price opened his own business in 1937 as a money manager for institutions and wealthy individuals.

In 1950, Price started his first growth stock mutual fund and also began managing money for the pension plan of a large corporation.

Until that time, pension funds had been managed for the most part by banks. Today, in addition to pension plans, a large percentage of T. Rowe Price Associates' assets consist of IRAs, Keoghs, 401(k) plans, and other retirement plans. With the aging of baby boomers, job insecurity, and the potential problems of Social Security, retirement plans have become a major force in the growth of the stock market and mutual funds.

In 1960, many investment professionals considered stocks of small, young companies too risky to buy because their future was unpredictable. Going against the conventional wisdom, Price started a fund to purchase companies in their early stages of growth. Believing that large profits could be made by buying small firms with the potential to become future business leaders, Price purchased Xerox, Texas Instruments, and others when they were still young companies.

In the mid-1960s, the United States was involved in the Vietnam War and Price predicted that higher inflation (detrimental to stocks) would result in a major bear market in future years. He reasoned that with the large U.S. budget deficit at that time and no increase in taxes to pay for the war, the costs would be paid in the form of accelerating inflation. Perceiving that the value of paper money would decrease and the value of hard assets increase due to high inflation, Price started another fund with the objective of protecting investments from inflation. In addition to growth stocks that he thought could keep up with inflation, Price bought stocks of companies owning and developing natural resources—metals, minerals, forest products, oil, and land. Among these companies were Atlantic Richfield (oil), Alcan Aluminum (aluminum), Homestake Mining Company (gold), and International Paper (forest products). His predictions about the stock market and inflation became reality when the Dow Jones Industrial Average dropped 45 percent between 1973 and 1974. In 1973, inflation was over 8 percent and, in 1974, over 12 percent.

Price said that investors should anticipate the changing of an era: "It is better to be too early than too late in recognizing the passing of one era, the waning of old investment favorites, and the advent of a new era affording new opportunities for the investor."

According to David Testa, chief investment officer of T. Rowe Price Associates, who worked with Price: "If he were investing today, Price would likely be intrigued with the Internet and recognize that it has ushered in a new era for consumers, businesses, and investors. Based on his criteria, Price would have bought established businesses that benefit from the Internet. Price also would have attempted to identify some future winners among Internet businesses if he could determine a price he believed was reasonable in relation to future potential earnings."[3]

Known for his articles on investing published in *Forbes* and *Barron's,* Price also wrote educational bulletins for his firm. T. Rowe Price Associates carries on this tradition, providing their investors with reports, investing guides, insight bulletins, and other valuable educational materials (an Insight Bulletin is included in Chapter 21).

Chapter 19

Price's Success Strategies: Think Like a Business Owner, but Be Aware That "Change Is the Investor's Only Certainty"

WHILE PRICE WAS developing his investment philosophy, he observed that great fortunes were made by people who retained ownership of their successful businesses over a long period of years: "The owners of businesses such as Black & Decker, Disney, DuPont, Eastman Kodak, Sears, and countless others were long-term investors. They did not attempt to sell out and buy back their ownerships of the business through the ups and downs of the business and stock market cycles." Applying the same general concept to stock ownership, Price developed a long-term buy-and-hold investment strategy.

"To identify profitable stocks requires only what my grandmother called gumption, my father called horse sense, and most people call common sense," Price remarked. "Buy stocks of growing businesses, managed by people of vision, who understand significant social and economic trends and who are preparing for the future through intelligent R&D," he advised. "Sell when the company no longer meets your buying criteria."

At times, companies have setbacks in earnings and stock prices fall. Price had the patience and discipline to hold companies during periods of lower earnings as long as he believed they would have future earnings growth and good management. In 1972, Price described his five best long-term performers, shown in the following table:

Increase in Value of Price's Long-Term Holdings

Company	Years Held	Percentage Increase	Annual Percentage Increase	Div. Yield*
Black & Decker	35	+ 8,540	+13.6	80.0%
Minnesota Mining	33	+17,025	+16.9	192.4
Merck & Company	31	+23,666	+16.9	293.3
Avon Products	17	+15,528	+35.6	154.3
Xerox	12	+ 6,184	+41.2	34.9

*Dividend yield based on original cost

How Price's Early Experiences Influenced His Investment Philosophy and Strategies

Price studied chemistry in college and a few years later he went to work as a chemist for E.I. DuPont. He was impressed with DuPont's R&D as well as the company's employee relations and benefits program. After studying DuPont's company reports and those of other companies, Price became fascinated with the business aspect of firms. He found studying economic trends, financial reports, and products and technologies of businesses so much more exciting than his job as a chemist that he decided the securities business was his true calling and went to work for a brokerage firm. As an investor, Price looked for stocks of firms with "intelligent R&D" (a track record of producing quality products) as well as good employee relations and benefits to attract and retain top-notch employees.

Two other positions that Price held before entering the investment field also helped shape his investment philosophy. One was at an enameling company that went bankrupt because of poor management and the other at a firm with executives who were not only incompetent but dishonest. Because of these experiences, Price made it a policy to find out as much as possible about the executives of companies he was considering buying.

Years later, in a memo to his firm, Price wrote: *"Every business is man-made. It results from the efforts of individuals. It reflects the personalities and business philosophy of the founders and those who have directed its affairs throughout its existence. If you want to have an understanding of any business, it is important to know the background of the people who started it and directed its past and the hopes and ambitions of those who are planing its future."*

Change Is the Investor's Only Certainty

"A successful investment philosophy must be flexible to cope with and anticipate changes," Price said. "Change is the investor's only certainty. Changing social, political, and economic trends as well as trends of industries and companies require change in the selection of shares in business enterprises."

Among Price's first stock purchases in the late 1930s were Dow Chemical, Coca-Cola, Minnesota Mining, and J.C. Penney. At the end of the 1940s, believing in the future of computers, Price purchased IBM, which became one of his biggest winners. In the 1960s, he added electronics firms and companies involved with space technology—Motorola and Texas Instruments. In the 1970s, with high inflation and interest rates, Price owned stocks of natural resource–related firms, as previously mentioned, and continued to hold growth companies—Avon Products, Black & Decker, General Electric, and Pfizer.

Now managing Price's original growth fund, Bob Smith of T. Rowe Price Associates has purchased some of the same stocks owned by Price. Unlike Price, who did not invest globally, Smith invests worldwide. In 1999, among Smith's global holdings were MCI Worldcom and Nokia. Cisco Systems, Dell Computer, Intel, and America Online were among stocks held in the technology and Internet sectors. Stocks in the financial sector were Wells Fargo, Aetna, and Citigroup. Consumer stocks included Warner-Lambert, Bristol-Myers Squibb, Pfizer, Gillette, and Procter & Gamble.

Chapter 20

Price Applies the 3 Steps: Examining the Growth and Life Cycles of Companies

Step 1: Gather the Information

Reading *The Wall Street Journal, The New York Times, Barron's, Forbes,* and other business publications helped Price find investment leads. He watched for new products and technologies, changing consumer and business trends, and news about political and economic policies that might affect businesses. Often, Price would clip and save articles of interest, then refer to them later.

He followed economic statistics and government policies relating to business. He analyzed changes in corporate profits, the balance of trade, the national debt, and the gross domestic product (GDP, formerly known as the gross national product, which measures the output of goods and services in the economy and indicates how much the economy is growing). Contemporary investors also look at economic surveys conducted by The Conference Board (www.conference-board.org). The Board reports results of its Consumer Confidence Index and Leading Economic Indicators, comprised of a variety of statistics such as unemployment claims and stock prices. Of course, Price paid attention to the rate of inflation and interest rates. He watched the Federal

Reserve Board (the Fed) and considered how its decisions regarding monetary policy and interest rates might affect his investments. Bloomberg Financial (www.bloomberg.com) and other research services report and comment on important policy changes of the Fed. Results of Fed meetings are widely reported in the press.

Lower inflation and interest rates are generally positive for stocks. But when inflation heats up and the Fed raises interest rates, this has a negative impact on stocks and can be poison for bonds, depending on how much and how often rates are raised. The Department of Labor (stats.bls.gov) reports the rate of inflation based on changes in the Consumer Price Index (CPI) and the Producer Price Indexes (PPI). The CPI measures changes in the prices of food, housing, apparel, transportation, medical care, and other goods and services. The PPI, a family of indexes, measures changes in prices by domestic producers of goods and services—flour, cotton, steel mill products, lumber, petroleum, natural gas, and other products.

Price studied annual reports, proxy statements, and other company reports. To help him determine the quality of management, he or analysts working with him interviewed top executives of purchase candidates.

Sources of information that can be used by investors following Price's strategies include *Value Line Investment Survey* (valueline. com), Market Guide (marketguide.com), and Yahoo! (yahoo.com) for researching companies. *Standard & Poor's Industry Surveys* (www. standardandpoor.com) contain background information, trends, and key financial ratios and statistics for many industries.

Infotrac (www.galegroup.com) and other databases, available in libraries and universities, can be used to research companies and the top executives who run them. Web sites such as *The Wall Street Journal*'s Interactive Edition (wsj.com), which has a link to the company briefing book containing past articles, also can be used to research a company's top executives. Forecasting services, such as Kiplinger reports (kiplinger.com) and H.S. Dent Forecast Newsletter (www. hsdent.com) provide and interpret data regarding consumer and business trends.

Step 2: Evaluate the Information

The investment criteria applied by Price is still used by analysts and money managers of T. Rowe Price Associates. To determine if a company met his criteria, Price would ask questions such as:

- Is management capable and reputable?
- Do the top executives and directors own a substantial amount of shares in the company?
- Are the business' products better than competitors' and in demand by customers?
- Does the firm have a track record of increasing sales, earnings, and dividends?
- Are profit margins favorable and sustainable?
- Is management earning a good return on the shareholders' equity and total invested capital?
- Does the company have a good credit rating with low or reasonable debt?
- Does the firm have intelligent R&D as evidenced by a track record of outstanding products?
- Is the company an industry leader with a competitive advantage?
- Does the company have good employee relations and benefits to attract and retain top-notch employees?
- Is the stock selling at a reasonable price relative to future potential earnings and the historical P/E?

Price strongly disliked government interference in business and, today, he would probably avoid firms like the tobacco companies for this and other reasons. Additionally, analysts and money managers of T. Rowe Price Associates look for companies that have strong free cash flows (see page 79, for more about free cash flows).

Intrinsic Value and P/Es

"The valuation of what a share of a business is worth as an investment is usually quite different from the market quotation because prices bear little relationship to intrinsic value of a company during periods when pessimism is overdone and during times when optimism is rampant," Price said. "Stock prices are affected by corporate earnings and dividends, the economy, inflation or deflation, and the psychology of investors."

Price cautioned: "Investors should be concerned about overpaying for stocks selling at high P/Es. Stocks go through periods when popularity with the public and institutional investors—mutual fund and pension plan managers—is high, so excessive demand causes prices to rise well above their investment value. This is usually a bad time to buy, but if an investor is anxious to invest in the business enterprise he [or she] may be justified in stretching buy limits. Investors should be prepared, having enough cash reserves, to increase ownership when the stocks are out of favor—the best time to buy any stock that qualifies as a purchase candidate."

Illustrating how P/Es can change during market fluctuations, Price gave two examples of purchases he made between 1968 and 1970.

Changing Stock Prices and P/Es, 1968–70

	High	P/E	Low	P/E
General Electric	50	25	30	17
Perkin Elmer*	29	62	9	15

*Perkin Elmer was acquired by EG&G in 1999.

Price bought General Electric at a P/E of 24, which was close to its high, but he felt the stock warranted this P/E. On the other hand, he purchased Perkin-Elmer at a P/E of 21, closer to its low. Price preferred to buy stocks close to or lower than the P/E of the general market and the stock's five-year historical average annual P/E. With the high volatility of current markets, it is not uncommon for stocks to sell at a wide range of P/Es.

"Generally, when bonds are paying high interest rates, P/Es of stocks are lower. Conversely, when interest paid by bonds are low, P/Es of stocks are higher," he wrote. "In a low interest rate, low inflation environment, it is easier for companies to generate higher earnings."

Evaluating Profit Margins and Variations among Stock Research Services

Price looked for well-run companies with sound financial controls and favorable profit margins. Profit margins are ratios, expressed as a percent, showing various relationships of sales (revenues) and earnings (profits or income). There are four main levels of profit margins for a business that investors may look at (also see "Financial Ratio Analysis," page 69):

1. Gross profit margin

2. Operating profit margin

3. Pretax profit margin

4. Net (after-tax) profit margin

Although he might look at the other three levels of profit margins, Price would focus on the operating profit margin. The operating profit margin shows the relationship of operating earnings (profits of the firm's main business as opposed to income from investments or other sources) to sales. To determine the trend of margins, Price compared a company's margins each year for five or more years. The next table contains year-to-year comparisons of operating profit margins for IBM, Microsoft, General Electric, and Pfizer from 1994 to 1998 as well as those of the industry in which they operate.

Year-to-Year Comparisons of Operating Profit Margins

Company	1998	1997	1996	1995	1994	Industry 1998
IBM	17.3	18.0	18.5	21.6	17.5	12.7
Microsoft	55.0	50.1	41.0	38.9	42.2	30.5
GE	21.2	19.0	18.3	18.0	17.4	15.2
Pfizer	30.2	30.8	31.0	29.3	27.3	28.3

Source: *Value Line Investment Survey*

It is important to be aware that definitions and calculations for ratios such as the operating profit margin can vary among stock research services. This explains why financial ratios for the same company may be different depending on the stock research service. Investors who use more than one service may determine the basis of the calculations by reading the glossary on the Web site or calling the customer support line. Value Line (valueline.com), for example, defines the operating margin as operating earnings before depreciation (a noncash deduction to allow for wear and tear and the aging of plants and equipment, as well as other noncash deductions), interest on debt, and taxes. To calculate the operating profit margin, Value Line divides operating earnings by sales.

Market Guide (marketguide.com), another respected source of financial information, provides several profit margins, which are explained on the company's Web site. A profit margin provided by Market Guide is referred to as EBITD—earnings before interest, taxes, and depreciation, which is the same as Value Line's operating profit margin. Market Guide also provides the operating profit margin, but includes depreciation.

$$\text{Operating Profit Margin} = \frac{\text{Operating Earnings}}{\text{Sales}}$$

The gross profit margin relates sales to the costs of sales. This margin shows how much of each sales dollar is left over after subtracting costs, such as raw materials and labor costs, directly incurred in generating sales. The gross profit margin is calculated by subtracting the cost of goods sold from total sales and dividing by total sales.

$$\text{Gross Profit Margin} = \frac{\text{Total Sales} - \text{Cost of Goods Sold}}{\text{Total Sales}}$$

The pretax profit margin relates earnings before taxes to sales. To calculate this ratio, divide pre-tax earnings by sales.

$$\text{Pre-Tax Margin} = \frac{\text{Pre-Tax Earnings}}{\text{Sales}}$$

The net profit margin indicates the relationship of after-tax earnings to sales and is calculated by dividing after-tax earnings by sales.

$$\text{Net Profit Margin} = \frac{\text{After-Tax Earnings}}{\text{Sales}}$$

The next table illustrates the four levels of profit margins for various companies with 1998 figures.

Four Levels of Profit Margins

Company	Gross	Operating	Pre-Tax	Net
GE	57.92	13.4	13.41	9.3
IBM	37.80	11.2	11.07	7.7
Microsoft	85.75	50.3	60.22	39.3
Pfizer	84.54	19.2	19.15	14.4

Source: Market Guide Statistics

Evaluating Return on Total Invested Capital

In addition to return on shareholder's equity (ROE) (discussed in Chapter 3), Price also evaluated the return on investment (ROI) ratio. It shows the return management has earned on total long-term capital, which includes shareholders' equity plus long-term debt. Companies can raise long-term capital by selling stock to shareholders, who benefit as earnings increase but also may suffer when earnings decline. To raise long-term capital, companies also may borrow money—long-term debt. Lenders benefit by having a stream of income from the interest paid by the company until the debt matures. The use of debt can increase ROE, but some conservative investors may prefer to see low debt. Borrowing money can be helpful in good times, but the outlay of money to pay interest on debt causes an extra burden for a firm in bad times when earnings decline.

Market Guide calculates ROI by dividing net earnings by total long-term capital (value of the common plus preferred stock plus long-term debt or any other long-term liabilities).

$$\text{Return on Investment} = \frac{\text{Net Earnings}}{\text{Total Long-Term Capital}}$$

Value Line looks at ROI another way—net earnings plus one half the interest charges on long-term debt divided by total capital (long-term debt plus shareholders' equity) expressed as a percentage. The resulting number, provided in Value Line's research reports can be compared with ROE to determine the impact of the use of borrowed capital to enhance the return to stockholders. Looking at the next table showing ROE and ROI for IBM and other companies, it is apparent that IBM has larger debt.

Company	Return on Shareholders' Equity ROE	Return on Total Invested Capital ROI
GE	23.9	23.5
IBM	32.6	18.6
Microsoft	28.8	28.8
Pfizer	29.9	28.4

Source: *Value Line Investment Survey*, 1998 numbers

Another ratio that investors may evaluate, along with ROE and ROI, is return on assets (ROA), which measures the percent management has earned on total assets. To calculate ROA divide net income by total assets.

$$\text{Return on Assets} = \frac{\text{Net Income}}{\text{Total Assets}}$$

These three ratios, ROE, ROI, and ROA, are indicators of how effectively management is using capital.

Benefits of Growing Dividends

There is less emphasis on dividends today than in Price's time and more on the wise use of retained earnings by corporate executives. Price usually bought companies that he thought had the potential to increase both dividends and earnings over time.

"Most individual and institutional investors have a dual objective: (1) current income and growth of income to provide for living and operating expenses and (2) increase in market value of invested capital to pay for rising cost of durable goods and other property," Price said. "According to the adage, 'A bird in the hand is worth two in the bush,' income, similar to the bird in the hand, is in possession and available to be used as desired. Increase in market value, similar to two birds in the bush, is not in possession until stocks are sold and the paper profits realized and turned into cash. Stock quotations are volatile. If one sells when market prices are high, the goal will have been accomplished. But if market prices decline and stocks have not been sold, capital gains diminish and may be lost entirely." Price pointed out that even in a future bull market, individual stocks may not reach their previous high prices.

"Too many people who invest in growth stocks are market conscious and fail to realize the importance of dividend income," Price observed. He warned: "If investors buy growth stocks near the top of a bull market, paying a high price with a low dividend yield (or paying no dividend), there is danger of losing the compounding effect of reinvested dividends. And there is also the danger of not having the dividend yield to offset possible losses when the market corrects. The degree of this danger depends on the depth and duration of the market downturn."

An example of how dividends can grow is Avon Products. Price purchased Avon in 1955, when the dividend per share was $0.04. By 1972, Avon's dividend had grown to $1.35 a share, an increase of 3,275 percent, or a compound annual growth rate of 23 percent.

During the 20 years from 1978 to 1998, reinvested dividends contributed over 50 percent of the investment returns of the Standard & Poor's 500 Index. According to statistics calculated by Wiesenberger, A Thomson Financial Company, a $10,000 initial investment in this Index grew to $127,868 without dividends; with dividends reinvested, it grew to $262,606.

Applying Criteria with Flexibility

Often, a stock will not fit all of an investor's criteria but still may qualify for purchase. Price might have bought a few stocks like Yahoo!, America Online, or other Internet companies. However, he probably would have tried to identify them early, before they became popular on Wall Street, and would have applied a modified version of his criteria. For these newer firms, Price might have looked for a huge potential market for products or services, a strong competitive advantage, growing sales, positive free cash flows or at least a strong cash position, and capable management.

In November 1999, Marc H. Gerstein, an equity analyst with the research service market guide (marketguide.com), wrote an article for the firm's Web site and said, "The modern Internet was just recently invented and it's normal for start-up companies in emerging businesses to spend more than they take in during the early years. So it's not reasonable to apply to this sector the sort of expectations that would be standard for blue-chip firms in businesses that have been around for decades."

It is also likely that Price would have owned firms such as Cisco Systems and Microsoft at some point. Price bought companies with low debt and a track record of outstanding products, as well as those with top executives who own a substantial amount of the firm's shares.

Bob Smith, manager of Price's original growth fund, comments on how Microsoft, a stock he has held, fits this criteria: "Bill Gates (CEO) has owned approximately 20 percent of Microsoft's stock and has had the ability to attract top-notch employees."[1] Microsoft has had no debt, high profit margins, and excellent returns on shareholders' equity.

Although Microsoft doesn't pay a dividend, Price might have made an exception regarding his criteria for dividends. But he strongly disliked government interference in business and no doubt would have been unhappy about the U.S. Justice Department's antitrust suit against Microsoft. In November 1999, Judge Thomas Penfield Jackson found that Microsoft was a monopoly and used its power to harm competition. After arbitration failed in 2000, the Justice Department recommended splitting Microsoft into two companies. As of spring 2000, how the case will affect Microsoft's future business is not clear (Microsoft will likely appeal).

Life Cycles of Companies and Earnings Growth Rate

"An understanding of the life cycle of earnings growth and judgment in appraising future earnings trends are essential to investing," Price said. He compared the life cycle of a company to that of a human—birth, maturity, and decline. After the birth of a company, growing business enterprises go through a start-up stage. Next, companies that survive this stage enter a dynamic stage of earnings growth, followed by mature growth with subsequent earnings slowdowns. And later, there is decline with no earnings growth.

Companies in the start-up stage may have small or negative earnings. When a business enters the dynamic growth stage, earnings can increase rapidly and be 100 percent or more. In recent years, some companies, such as those dominating the technology field, have continued to show relatively high growth rates for a long period. Two of these firms are Cisco Systems and Microsoft. Founded in 1984, Cisco Systems' average annual compounded earnings growth rate was about 59 percent for the five years ending 1998 (based on Value Line's statistics). Microsoft, incorporated in 1975, had an average annual compounded earning growth rate of 34.5 percent for the same period. As companies grow larger and older, earnings growth may slow to between 7 percent and 15 percent. For the past five years, General Electric, established in 1878, has had an average annual compounded earnings growth rate of about 13 percent; and Coca-Cola, incorporated in 1892, about 15 percent (based on Value Line's statistics).

In the declining stage, businesses may show no earnings growth or negative earnings and eventually go out of business. But some companies revitalize or reinvent themselves by finding new markets, products, policies, or concepts to create growth. In 1960, S.S. Kresge, a chain of variety stores reporting low earnings, ranked third in its industry after Woolworth and W. T. Grant. Management decided to try a new concept and renamed the firm Kmart Corporation. W.T. Grant went into bankruptcy and ceased doing business, but Kmart remained in business. Motorola is another company that has refocused and reinvented itself (covered in Chapter 15).

Dollar Amount of Sales and Unit Sales

When Price bought stocks or monitored holdings, he paid attention to the dollar amount of sales as well as unit sales and earnings reported by the firm. This helped him to evaluate the stage of a company's growth. Sales can be reported in two ways: (1) total amount of sales in dollars and (2) unit sales. In the automobile industry, unit sales means the number of cars and trucks sold; for utilities, kilowatt hours; for airlines, passenger miles.

Price would ask, "Is the company increasing sales by selling more products or services, by raising prices, or both?" Generally, there is a limit as to how much a firm can raise prices without customers looking for a substitute product. This is especially true in today's competitive markets. So it is important to look at unit sales as well. Coca-Cola and other firms report unit sales in company reports. Coca-Cola's unit sales are reported by a unit case—24 eight fluid ounce servings. Unit sales also may be found in Value Line reports, on industry commentary pages, and through other research services.

Companies that have multiple product lines may not report unit sales. For these firms, Price might call the CFO or determine through other research whether the bulk of sales was due to price increases or to selling more products. To obtain this information, investors may call a firm's CFO or speak with representatives in the investor relations department of a firm.

"Stocks should be monitored to detect changes in earnings growth," according to Price. He considered decreases in unit sales and dollar volume sales, coupled with lower earnings, a warning sign of slowing growth.

Price pointed out: "The fact that a company fails to show earning growth each year is no assurance that earning growth has ceased. Business cycles and developments within an industry or company frequently distort the reported earnings pattern for a period of one or more years. It requires experienced research and alert judgment to detect the basic change in the earnings cycle."

In addition to lower sales and earnings, some of the warning signs that Price cited were lower profit margins and lower return on invested capital or return on shareholders' equity for several quarters. This information can be found in company reports and stock research reports.

Writing for *Barron's* in 1939, Price said that the railroad industry had reported a decline in ton miles for a period of years and compared this with the utility industry, which was still growing in kilowatt hours. Price was not in favor of buying stocks of utility companies at the time he wrote this article because the government was imposing burdensome controls. He might, however, be buying some utility companies today. David Testa, chief investment officer of T. Rowe Price Associates, says that a current example of an industry with declining unit sales is the defense industry. Companies in the defense industry have lost business due to cutbacks in military spending by the U.S. government.

A Company's Size Makes a Difference

A company's size may be defined by its sales, but to investment professionals the term *size* generally means market capitalization (market cap) calculated by multiplying the price of a stock by the number of shares outstanding. Companies are categorized as small, medium (mid), or large.

There are no specific industry-wide standards to define cutoff points of small, medium, and large companies. According to T. Rowe Price Associates, companies with market caps of $500 million are considered small, over $5 billion, large, and firms that fall in the middle are mid-caps. Small, emerging growth companies, sometimes called micro-caps may have a total market cap of between $50 million and $500 million.

Although Price invested in large companies such as General Electric, Coca-Cola, and others, he also bought smaller firms that he thought had great future growth potential. Small companies are usually traded on the Nasdaq and their stocks can be extremely volatile. Often, there is less information available about smaller firms and they require more research.

A great deal of money has been made by investors who bought successful companies in their early stages of growth, when they were small, and held for the longer term. Large sums of money have been lost by those who invested heavily in small companies that turned out to be land mines instead of gold mines. It is especially important to evaluate the financial strength and debt requirements of small companies to make sure they can weather financial storms that may occur as they are growing up. In addition, David Testa says, "Investors have to consider whether the firm has worthwhile products and if there is a large enough market for these products to create good future growth."

Price started a mutual fund in 1960 with the objective of buying the stocks of small growth firms. For a few years after the fund's inception, performance was poor. In 1962, when the Standard & Poor's 500 Index was off 9 percent, Price's fund dropped 29 percent. Although he was disappointed, Price stayed with it and performance improved. Five years later, the fund gained 44 percent in comparison to an increase of 9 percent for the Index. By 1968, small growth stocks were hot and the money poured in so quickly, Price had to close the fund temporarily to protect shareholders. He didn't want to be under pressure to make investments when stock prices were at such high levels.

In the 1960s, Price purchased Xerox and Texas Instruments when they were still small-cap companies. Sun Microsystems, Home Depot,

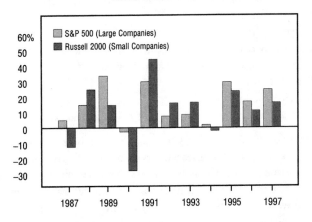

Small-Company vs Large-Company Stocks

Annual Returns: 1987–1997

Source: T. Rowe Price Associates Insight Bulletin, *Investing in Small-Company Stocks*

and Microsoft were the small-cap companies of the 1980s that became the success stories of the 1990s. There are times when small companies, as a group, have performed better than larger companies and the reverse, as illustrated in the above chart. A well-selected small company, however, may perform well, even when most small-cap firms do not. Some investors try to identify small firms with dynamic growth that will become the household names of the future. For others, the best way to invest in small companies is to buy a mutual fund with a proven track record of success that owns small companies.

Step 3: Make the Decision

Prior to buying a stock, Price would make sure the company met his criteria, listed on page 134. To monitor companies, he paid attention to earnings and sales growth as well as changes in profit margins and return on invested capital or return on shareholders' equity. According to Price, warning signals and problems potentially contributing to slowing grow include:

- Decreasing sales
- Declining earnings and profit margins for several quarters
- Lower return on invested capital for several quarters
- Sharply increasing taxes
- Negative changes in management
- Potentially detrimental government interference or unfavorable court decisions (of a substantial nature)
- Saturation of markets
- Increasing competition
- Substantial increases in the cost of raw materials and labor

Information for monitoring stocks can be found through reading company reports and stock research service reports. Current newspaper or magazine articles about a firm or stock research reports may contain information about increasing competition, saturation of markets, and government actions potentially detrimental to a firm.

Aware that firms would have slowdowns due to industry weakness or the economy, he compared earnings of his holdings with competitors' earnings and with growth in the overall economy. This helped him find distortions due to business cycles of recessions and recoveries and to determine the real trends in earnings.

Scale Buying and Selling

"When a bear market drove prices down to our predetermined buy limits, we had no idea how far they would go, when they would recover, or how far they would advance," Price said. "But we knew we wanted to become long-term shareowners of attractive stocks of business enterprises. We used scale buying and selling."

During a declining market, for instance, Price might put in an order to buy a stock at $45 a share, buy more at $42, and buy again at $40. Of course, the market could have gone against him and he might not have been able to accumulate all the stock he wanted. During a bull market, when Price wanted to reduce holdings in a stock or sell, he placed orders at a predetermined price and subsequent orders at higher prices. If the general market or the stock began falling, or adverse news about the company was announced, the remaining shares to be sold were liquidated at the market (the order is entered with no price limit and is sold at the current market price).

Declines in stock prices did not cause Price to sell. If he thought a firm had favorable future prospects, it was an opportunity to buy more. Price sold stocks when he believed future growth would not continue or if a company no longer met his buying criteria. He would also sell a stock to raise cash for an investment that he considered a better value than one of his holdings, taking into consideration the costs of selling and taxes.

Consider the Tax Implications of Selling Investments

Investors may be able to offset some of the taxes on stock profits with losses or other deductions, but "capital gains taxes are a penalty for highly successful investors," Price said. He cited Avon as an example: "The stock cost less than $1 a share and some of the stock was sold at $131 a share, so the capital gains was approximately $130. Federal and state taxes vary with the individual's tax bracket and the amount of capital gains realized. With a capital gains tax of 30 percent [today the maximum capital gains tax rate is 20 percent], after deducting the 30 percent from $131, or $39, only $92 remains for reinvestment. If this is reinvested in another growth stock, the purchase would have to increase approximately 44 percent to recover the tax paid before breaking even by the switch."

Sell Avon at	$131		Proceeds of Sale of Avon	$131
Cost	$ 1		– Capital Gains Tax	$ 39
Capital Gain $130 × .30 = $39 Tax			Profit after Tax	$ 92

Chapter 21

Applying Price's Strategies for Different Types of Investors

PRICE HELPED CLIENTS allocate their money between stocks, bonds, and cash. He realized that needs for preservation of capital, high current income, and capital appreciation vary. "Each portfolio should have an investment program tailor-made to fit the objective of the individual investor, based on his [or her] requirements for safety of principal, spendable income, or capital growth," according to Price. "In the capital growth portion of a portfolio (stocks), risk should be minimized by broad industry and company diversification."

To help his clients determine their real objectives, Price asked questions. "Do you want to safeguard your principal so that it can be turned into cash with little or no loss at any time, regardless of whether markets for bonds and stocks are up or down (capital preservation—the stability of principal and income)? Do you want safety of income at a fixed rate to meet current expenses (income)? Are you looking for profits or growth in market value of invested principal and higher income for the future (growth)?"

A comprehensive asset allocation program would take into consideration real estate ownership, commodities, and collectibles such as art, gold, silver, and other assets. For purposes of this discussion, however, asset allocation is limited to stocks, bonds, and cash.

Column A: Stocks (Investments for Growth)

Investment choices can be likened to a restaurant menu. Column A consists of investments for growth (individual and professionally managed stocks of small, medium, and large companies).

1. Domestic stocks

2. International stocks

3. Stock mutual funds
   - Domestic
   - Global (domestic and international stocks)
   - International
   - Index funds (funds that mimic an index such as the Standard & Poor's 500)

4. Variable annuities—insurance contracts with values based on sub-accounts (similar to mutual funds) performance

5. Privately managed stock accounts

Column B: Bonds and Other Fixed Income Investments (Investments with Emphasis on Income)

Column B includes individual and professionally managed investments with emphasis on income—bonds and other fixed income investments.

1. Domestic bonds

2. International bonds

3. Bond mutual funds (domestic)
   - Government
   - Corporate
   - Municipal

4. Bond mutual funds (international)
   - Government
   - Corporate

5. Privately managed bond accounts

6. Fixed interest rate annuities issued by insurance companies

Risks of Bond Investing

Bonds offer diversification and a source of additional income for investors who buy stocks; however, it is important to be aware of the risks of bond investing. Rising interest rates are usually negative for stocks and can be even more detrimental for bonds. When interest rates rise, bond prices fall. This occurs because an existing bond's fixed interest payments (at the lower rate) are not as attractive as bond yields with the new, higher fixed interest payments. Conversely, when interest rates fall, bond prices go up as bonds paying higher interest become more attractive. Suppose, for example, an investor purchased a $1,000 bond paying 7 percent interest, maturing in 30 years. If interest rates decline to 6 percent, new bonds will have lower yields. The bond paying 7 percent becomes more attractive to other investors and its price would increase. But if interest rates rise, the 7 percent bond is less attractive and its price decreases (for more about investing in bonds, see "What You Should Know about Bonds" at the end of this chapter).

Column C: Cash Equivalents (Investments for Capital Preservation—Stability of Principal and Income)

Column C contains short-term (maturing in five years or less) cash equivalents, investments that can easily be converted to cash.

1. Bank accounts
   - Certificates of deposit (CDs)
   - Money market accounts

2. Money market mutual funds

3. Treasury bills

4. High-grade short-term bonds

Investing in Cash Equivalents

Investing in cash equivalents may appear to be risk-free, but there can be some danger involved. For example, one risk for buyers of bank certificates of deposit (CDs) is that interest rates change from time to time and a CD buyer may receive more or less income in future years. In 1980, banks were paying as much as 16 percent for six-month CDs. In 1987, six-month CDs paid about 8 percent, and in 1993, six-month CDs paid 3 percent. That means that someone who bought a six-month bank CD for $100,000 in 1980 had an annualized income of $16,000; in 1987, $8,000; and in 1993, only $3,000. As of December 1999, six-month CDs were paying about 4.5 percent.

Asset Allocation Strategies for Different Types of Investors

Generally, it is recommended that conservative investors purchase financially strong large or mid-size companies, and own smaller companies in the form of mutual funds. Conservative investors can participate in global markets through multinational U.S. firms or buy mutual funds that invest globally.

Moderate and aggressive investors have wide investment choices, depending on their experience and knowledge. These investors may own individual stocks of smaller companies and mutual funds holding small-cap stocks. They may also own foreign stocks in addition to global and international mutual funds (covered in Chapter 28).

The question of how much money to allocate to each of the three columns has been debated and answered in different ways. There are comprehensive computerized asset allocation programs and simple one-size-fits-all answers. A simple formula is to subtract an investor's age from 100, which is then expressed as the percent to be allocated to stocks and the rest in bonds and cash reserves. This means someone age 20 would have 80 percent in stocks; age 50, 50 percent in stocks; and age 80, 20 percent in stocks. Conceptually, younger people have more time for stocks to grow, can take more risk, and can tolerate more volatility. But some young investors are conservative and prefer to own more investments from columns B and C. Affluent older investors may be more aggressive and own more from column A. Some wealthy people in their seventies and eighties invest for their children and grandchildren, acting as custodians of the next generation's money.

Asset Allocation and an Investor's Time Horizon

Price recommended that investments be aligned with the investor's goals, risk tolerance, and time horizon. If an investor has a short-term goal of a major purchase such as a car or a house in the next two years, the obvious choice would be investments from column C—cash equivalents that offer stability of principal. An investor with an intermediate-term goal, for instance, paying for a child's education in five years, may choose cash equivalents from column C as well as short- or intermediate-term bonds from column B. An investor planing for retirement in 10 or 20 years would be looking for growth and would choose more investments from column A but could buy investments from any column, depending on his or her risk tolerance.

Asset allocation should be a personal decision, reflecting goals, income needs, time horizon, and an investor's experience, knowledge, and attitude toward various investments. It is advisable to work with an investment professional to create a comprehensive asset allocation plan.

The Power of Compound Growth

Like the famous scientist, Albert Einstein, who considered compound interest one of the wonders of the world, Price also marveled at the power of compound interest.

Price commented: "Money invested at a fixed rate of interest compounded over a period of years increases or grows in value at a predetermined rate. The higher the interest rate, the faster the increase or rate of growth in the value of the invested capital. Most people are familiar with compound interest and how it works. For the investor, at high rates over a long period of years, compound interest can create a fortune. Invested capital with interest compounded at 7.2 percent doubles in a ten-year period (100 percent increase). During a 20-year period, it increases over 300 percent. In 30 years, it increases over 700 percent. In 40 years, it increases over 1,500 percent. Invested capital with interest compounded at 15 percent increases over 300 percent in ten years. During a 20-year period, it increases over 1,500 percent. In 30 years, it increases over 6,500 percent. In 40 years, it increases 26,686 percent." This concept is illustrated below.

How Money Grows—$10,000 Compounded at 7.2 Percent and 15 Percent

Years	Growth at 7.2 Percent	Growth at 15 Percent
10	$ 20,000	$ 40,000
20	40,000	161,300
30	80,000	622,110
40	161,300	2,678,000

"Capital invested in a share of a company experiencing the same rate of [compound] growth in market value will produce similar results," said Price. "For example, when I bought Avon it sold at $0.875 a share in 1955. At the end of 1972, it was worth $136 a share. This is an increase of 15,528 percent or a compound annual growth of 34.6 percent. The dividend paid in 1955 was $0.04. In 1972, it was $1.35. This is an increase of 3,275 percent or a compound annual growth of 23 percent. If one understood the fabulous results of compound growth over a period of decades, he or she would not be so anxious to try to make a killing by playing the ups and downs in the stock market. The growth stock theory of investing requires patience, but it is less stressful than trading, generally has less risk, and reduces brokerage commissions and income taxes."

The following is from a T. Rowe Price Insight Bulletin and relates to the previous discussion about bonds on pages 149 and 150.

What You Should Know about Bonds[1]

Bonds Represent Loans Made to Various Borrowers

While stocks are shares of ownership in a corporation, bonds are debt securities (IOUs) issued by borrowers to lenders (investors). They represent a promise made by borrowers to pay interest throughout the term of the loan and repay the amount of the loan on a certain date.

What distinguishes bonds from other fixed income securities is the length of time the loan remains in effect. Treasury bills and other money market securities mature in a year or less. Bonds have longer-term maturities. All sorts of borrowers, including the U.S. government, states, and municipalities, and corporations, issue bonds.

Fixing Your Sights on Fixed Income

The interest paid on bonds is usually a fixed dollar amount, but it can also vary in the case of variable rate securities. However, many investors confuse the coupon rate with the bond's actual yield and also its average annual compound rate of return when held to maturity (yield-to-maturity). You should understand the differences before you invest.

- *Coupon Rate.* The coupon rate is expressed as a percentage of par value, normally $1,000. Since most bonds pay interest semiannually, a bond with an 8% coupon rate will pay you $40 twice a year, for a total of $80 per year ($1,000 × .08 = $80). The coupon rate on a particular type of security ordinarily rises as maturities lengthen and also as the credit quality decreases. Among taxable investments, U.S. Treasury securities carry the lowest coupon rates because the federal government is the nation's most creditworthy borrower.
- *Current Yield.* While the coupon rate is fixed, the current yield fluctuates with rising and falling interest rates. A bond paying $80 interest per year yields 8% at par value. But if interest rates rose causing the bond's price to fall to $900, the yield would rise to 8.9%; had the price risen to a premium over par, say to $1,100, the yield would have dropped to 7.3%. You can easily figure out the current yield by dividing the interest paid each year by the current price of the bond.
- *Yield-to-Maturity.* If you hold a bond until it matures, the bond's compound annual rate of return is made up of two components: interest income and capital gain or loss. An 8% bond, bought at a price of $900 and held until it matures in 10 years would generate income of $800 and a capital gain of $100. Your average annual return, assuming all interest payments are reinvested at the same rate, is called the yield-to-maturity. You can get this yield from your broker or figure it out yourself with the help of a calculator.

Bond Prices Move in the Opposite Direction from Interest Rates

Since a bond's coupon is fixed, its price must move up and down with changes in interest rates in order to keep its yield in line with current rates. If you bought a bond with an 8% coupon and rates subsequently rose to 10% for similar bonds, your bond would normally decline in price to offer a yield close to the new rate to attract new investors.

The table below shows how values of bonds with various maturities change when interest rates rise or fall by one percentage point. The table assumes a 6% coupon and $1,000 par value for each bond.

Bond Maturity in Years	Rates fall 1% and the bond's value rises to . . .	Rates rise 1% and the bond's value drops to . . .
1	$1,009.63	$990.50
3	1,027.50	973.36
5	1,043.76	958.40
10	1,077.90	928.90
30	1,154.50	875.30

Source: T. Rowe Price Associates
The chart is for illustrative purposes only and does not represent the performance of any T. Rowe Price investment. The example shows value changes apart from fluctuations caused by other market conditions.

A bond's *duration*, rather than its maturity, is a better measure of the way interest rate swings affect bond prices. Duration takes into account the time value of cash flows generated over the life of a bond, discounting future interest and principal payments to arrive at a value expressed in years. So, the price of a bond with a duration of five years can be expected to rise about 5% for each one percentage point drop in interest rates, and fall about 5% for each one percentage point rise in rates.

Lending Your Money to the Country's Largest Institutions

Borrowing and lending money is a major business, made up of a wide array of borrowers and lenders. The primary issuers of debt securities in the U.S. include:

- *The U.S. Government.* Treasury bonds and bonds issued by the Government National Mortgage Association (Ginnie Maes or GNMAs) are backed by the full faith and credit of the U.S. government and represent the lowest risk of default.

  In addition, while bonds issued by various government-sponsored enterprises are not direct obligations of the U.S. Treasury, they are generally regarded as having the "moral" backing of the U.S. government and, therefore, carry a low credit risk. These include securities issued by the Federal National Mortgage Association (Fannie Mae), the Federal Home Loan Mortgage Corporation (Freddie Mac), the Federal Farm Credit Bank, and the Federal Home Loan Bank. The interest on U.S. Treasuries and some agency bonds is exempt from state and local income taxes, but not from federal taxes.

- *States and Local Municipalities.* State and local governments are heavy issuers of bonds (municipal bonds or "munis"). Their credit ratings vary according to the borrower's credit-worthiness, but they have historically experienced low default rates. The highest ratings are usually assigned to general obligation (GO) bonds, which are backed by the taxing power of the state or local government. Revenue bonds, issued to finance various public projects, are another large component of this market.

  The interest on most municipal bonds is exempt from federal income tax and also from state and local taxes if you invest in bonds within your home state. However, the income from some bonds issued to finance private projects, such as airports and sports facilities, may be subject to the alternative minimum tax (AMT). Also, any profit realized from the sale of munis bought at a discount from par (except for those originally issued at a discount) may be taxed as ordinary income rather than as a capital gain. Therefore, you should check with your tax adviser before investing in private purpose or market discount bonds.

- *Corporations.* Companies issue bonds to finance various operations as an alternative to issuing stock. Bonds sold to the public by blue chip corporations enjoy higher credit ratings than other corporate bonds. Companies must pay interest on their bonds before paying dividends to stockholders. In the event of bankruptcy or liquidation of the company, bondholders also have priority over shareholders. Therefore, investment-grade corporate bonds (see the next chart) are generally regarded as less risky and less volatile than stocks.

Most major corporations, including utilities, financial, and industrial companies, issue some form of bonds. Some of these bonds may be *convertible* into shares of common stock, giving them potential for capital appreciation. Some corporate bonds are secured by assets of the company, while others are unsecured *debentures,* backed only by the creditworthiness of the issuing corporation.

Rating the Borrowers

The credit ratings of bonds are important because they largely determine how much incremental interest bond issuers must pay to borrow money and also provide investors with a measure of credit risk. The two major rating agencies are Standard & Poor's and Moody's, which have similar but not identical rating systems.

Moody's and Standard & Poor's Rating Codes

These rating systems are similar, although not identical. The chart is the key to reading the ratings.

	Moody's	S&P's	Meaning
Investment-Grade Bonds	Aaa	AAA	Highest-quality bonds. Issuers are considered extremely stable and dependable.
	Aa	AA	High-quality bonds. Long-term investment risk is slightly higher than on AAA bonds.
	A	A	Bonds with many favorable investment attributes.
	Baa	BBB	Medium-grade bonds. Quality is adequate at present, but long-term stability may be doubtful.
High-Yield Bonds	Ba B	BB B	Bonds with a speculative element. Security of payments is not well safeguarded.
	Caa Ca C	CCC CC C	Bonds are extremely speculative. The danger of a default is high.
	—	D	In default.

Bond yields reflect a borrower's ability to make timely payments of interest and principal. Therefore, U.S. Treasury bonds generally have lower yields than agency and corporate bonds with similar maturities. Likewise, investment-grade corporate bonds yield less than high-yield (noninvestment-grade) bonds because of their higher credit quality. Municipal bonds have lower yields than taxable bonds to reflect their tax advantages, but the credit quality of individual munis determines their relative yields within the tax-exempt sector.

You should also know that high-yield bonds sometimes perform more like stocks than like investment-grade bonds. While bonds usually rise and fall with fluctuations in interest rates, high-yield bonds are vulnerable to adverse economic trends and shortfalls in corporate earnings. These bonds have a much greater risk of default and tend to be more volatile and less liquid than higher-rated bonds.

Buying and Selling Bonds in a Competitive Marketplace

- *Treasuries.* While you need a minimum of $10,000 to buy bills and $5,000 to buy notes maturing in less than five years, bonds and notes with maturities of five years or longer can be purchased in denominations of $1,000.

  You have the option of buying Treasuries from brokerage firms, government securities dealers, some banks, or directly from the Federal Reserve at regularly scheduled auctions. New issues with maturities longer than 10 years are auctioned quarterly in February, May, August, and November. Of course, you can buy them in the *secondary market* at prevailing market prices whenever you like.
- *Municipals.* Munis are normally available in minimum denominations of $10,000, regardless of maturity. Liquidity varies with the nature of the obligation and the credit quality. However, the spread between bid and ask prices can be greater for transactions below $100,000. The payment of interest and principal on some municipal bonds is insured by private muni bond insurers, which supplies them with additional credit enhancement.
- *Corporates.* You can buy most corporate bonds in denominations of $1,000, either in the secondary market or at par

when the bonds are first issued. A small percentage of bonds, known as *baby bonds,* have been issued in smaller units of less than $1,000 par value.

Like stocks, corporate bonds are *listed* or *unlisted.* The more actively traded bonds of major corporations are listed on the New York and American bond exchanges, and you can track their prices in the financial pages of leading newspapers. However, the vast majority are unlisted and trade over the counter via telephone or computer negotiations between dealers. You have to call your broker for price quotes.

While many municipal and corporate bonds are callable, meaning that the issuer has the right to redeem them prior to maturity, only a small percentage of Treasury bonds have call features. [It is important to be aware of call provisions; you might have to reinvest the proceeds at a lower interest rate if your bond is called.]

Determining the Best Types of Bonds for You

What are the best kind of bonds for you? That depends on a number of factors, including your investment objectives, your income, and the level of risk you are willing to assume. The two major types of risk are market and credit risk.

- *Market Risk.* We discussed earlier how much a bond's price would rise or fall in response to a change in interest rates. One of the major risks you face as a bond investor is that interest rates will rise after you buy a bond, causing its price to fall. If you are prepared to hold your bond to maturity, this risk is eliminated.
- *Credit Risk.* This is the risk that a bond issuer will default—fail to make timely payments of interest and principal. The higher the credit quality, the lower the risk. If the creditworthiness of the issuer declines after you buy a bond, its price will likely fall to provide a higher yield to attract new investors, and you could take a loss on your investment. Also, lower credit quality bonds tend to be less liquid than higher-rated bonds.

Be Sure to Weigh All the Risks

You should weigh the inherent risks of each type of bond before you invest. "Reaching for yield," that is, buying bonds because they pay the highest amount of interest, is often a fundamental mistake of bond investors because high yields usually mean greater risk.

Before buying bonds, consider the following checklist:

- *Time Horizon.* How long will you be holding your bonds? You can control market risk to a great extent by "laddering" maturities—buying bonds with short, intermediate, and longer maturities. Keep in mind that the longer the maturity, the more vulnerable a bond is to changes in interest rates.
- *Tax Bracket.* Whether you should own taxable or tax-exempt bonds depends on your tax bracket. The best approach is to figure out your net yield on taxable (or partly tax-exempt) bonds after federal, state, and local income taxes are accounted for and compare it with the yield you would receive on tax-exempt securities.
- *Diversification.* Diversifying your holdings works as well with bonds as with stocks. By dividing your fixed income assets among various types of bonds with different maturities, you reduce your overall level of risk and the volatility of your portfolio as well.

Understand that bonds provide a balance to stocks and should complement them in most portfolios. They provide steady income and are less volatile under normal conditions. For investors with short time horizons and low tolerance for risk, fixed income securities should be the primary investment vehicle. The amount of income you want, the length of time you need it for, and the level of risk you are willing to assume to obtain it are all factors in determining the makeup of your fixed income investments.

Chapter 22

Current and Future Investment Trends: Technology, Health Care, and Financial Services

IN THE PAST decade, some of the fastest-growing firms have been in consumer products, Internet-related companies, technology, health care, and financial services.[1]

Technology

A T. Rowe Price Insight Bulletin discussing technology stocks began: "When Star Trek's Captain Kirk said space was the 'final frontier,' he overlooked a number of uncharted territories right here on earth. Modern science and technology is boldly going where no earthling has gone before."

New technologies will emerge in the future, according to T. Rowe Price portfolio manager, Charles Morris. However, several trends will continue to benefit companies in the technology field. One trend is the Internet's continuing contribution to the growth of technology firms that provide infrastructure, software, and communications gear. Another is continued growth in computer-related companies, which have benefited due to the expansion of computers from vehicles for data input and computation to communication and commerce, and from businesses to homes. Growth of wireless communication networks should also continue providing opportunities for business in this area. Among companies in the technology field are Lucent Technologies, Motorola, Texas Instruments, Microsoft, Novell, Oracle, Intel, Dell Computer, and Cisco Systems.

Health Care

Life expectancy has increased, and as people get older, they usually spend more on health care. According to the U.S. Department of Commerce, Census Bureau the average life expectancy in 1900 was 47 years; in 1950, 68 years; and in 1991, 75 years. Today, it is even higher. Expenditures for health care have been rising worldwide, as shown in the next table.

Health Care Expenditures as a Percentage of Gross Domestic Product

	1992	2002
United States	14.3	17.0
Canada	10.0	12.1
France	9.4	10.0
Germany	8.7	9.5
Japan	6.9	8.0
United Kingdom	7.1	8.0

Source: T. Rowe Price Insight Bulletin: Investing in Health Care

About one-third of U.S. health care spending has been attributed to Americans age 65 and older. The number of Americans in this age category is projected to double in the next 30 years.

The health care industry is attractive for investors, but problems include potential cost controls and regulation by federal and state governments as well as the Food and Drug Administration. Pharmaceutical companies with patented drugs that have been prime beneficiaries of rising health care spending face competition from producers of generic drugs when patents expire. The health care industry also consists of firms selling vitamins or other nutritional supplements, companies owning hospitals, nursing homes, health care facilities, businesses producing and selling laboratory equipment, and manufacturers and marketers of personal care products. Among the firms that have benefited from health care spending are Bristol-Myers Squibb, Pfizer, American Home Products, Johnson & Johnson, Biogen, Warner-Lambert, and United Heath Care.

Financial Services

Prior to the early 1990s, stocks of financial service companies (banks, mortgage and credit card companies, brokerage firms, mutual funds companies, and insurance firms) had high dividends and sold at low P/Es and low price-to-book value. Investors would buy these stocks for income and some growth. The financial services sector is now considered a growth industry and popular stocks in this sector may sell at higher P/Es and price-to-book value, with lower dividend yields. Aging baby boomers investing and saving for retirement, declining interest rates, new products, and mergers and acquisitions are factors that have contributed to the growth of the industry. Some companies that have participated in this growth are Citicorp, Travelers Group, Wells Fargo, Washington Mutual, Morgan Stanley Dean Witter, T. Rowe Price Associates, Fannie Mae, and Freddie Mac.

Chapter 23

The Life and Career of Thomas Rowe Price[1]

PRICE WAS BORN in 1898 in Glyndon, Maryland. His father was a country doctor who delivered more babies than any other doctor in the area. After graduating high school, Price attended Swarthmore where he majored in chemistry. He worked for several companies before deciding that he really wanted to become a money manager. Price's first job was as a chemist, with an enameling company. Decades later, in a memo to employees of T. Rowe Price Associates, Price described his experience: "This company, which had just been organized, was run by a couple of recent college graduates. I was green and inexperienced and took the job because I liked the young Princeton graduate who interviewed me. As it turned out, management was lacking in experience, the company was financially weak, and labor relations were bad. Within a month or so after I joined the organization, all the employees went out on strike and the company went out of business."

Price had another unpleasant experience with an employer who turned out to be dishonest. Price said that this taught him to be critical and skeptical, and he learned to scrutinize management carefully before making investments.

Although he was trained as a chemist, Price found studying financial reports, products and technologies of firms, and political and economic trends more exciting. Subsequently, he took a job with a brokerage firm. Price worked with clients and wrote a stock market letter. He was disturbed by some practices of the other brokers and complained about their use of high-pressure tactics to sell stocks. Rather then relying on his firm's recommendations, Price used his judgment in choosing the best investments for his clients.

"*Regardless of the immediate profit to me and instead of discussing just the good points about a stock, I also gave the bad side [the risks] of an investment,*" said Price. His investment strategy was to buy well-managed companies developing new products or technologies with great profit potential. Unlike the other brokers who thought stocks should be bought and sold for quick profits, Price believed stocks should be selected carefully and held for the long term.

In addition to the regular brokerage business, Price suggested to the principals of his firm that they create a separate fee-based money management division. He further recommended that the firm provide a service to structure portfolios for clients. To accomplish this, Price helped clients determine their investment profiles and recommended an appropriate allocation strategy among stocks, bonds, and cash equivalents. He was one of the first money managers to create a written asset allocation process.

John Legg, his boss and mentor, agreed to let him put his ideas into practice and started a new division of the firm. Price hired two assistants, Isabella Craig and Marie Walper, and two Harvard Business School graduates, Walter Kidd and Charles Shaeffer, who worked as analysts. Later when Price opened his own firm, Kidd and Shaeffer became his partners. Kidd had a talent for investigating new companies. Shaeffer was skilled in management and marketing. Profits from Price's money management division were small. Legg supported him, but other executives of the firm did not believe in his ideas.

Price remarked: "They did not fully comprehend my definition of growth stocks. Money was made more easily and quickly (and I might add lost) in dealing in securities [short-term buying and selling]." A few years later, Price was informed that the money management division was going to be closed and he would have to go back to working as a broker.

Price Starts a Money Management Business and His First Mutual Fund

After consulting with friends and other financial professionals, Price decided to start his own money management business and resigned from the firm. Focused on making his company a success, he sometimes worked as many as 16 hours a day. He offered prospective clients a trial period at no cost to manage their money. If they liked the results, they would pay a fee to continue his service.

Price, his two assistants, and Shaeffer and Kidd, who were working with him in this new endeavor, took substantially reduced salaries. To compensate, Price gave them stock in the company, which turned out to be quite profitable. T. Rowe Price Associates became a public company in 1986. In 1987, the stock of T. Rowe Price Associates sold at a low of $1.25 and in 1998, at a high of about $43 (adjusted for four stock splits).

The firm grew and Price became nationally known for his investment philosophy through articles he wrote for *Barron's*. In 1950, Price started his first mutual fund. The rules regarding estate taxes were different from today; $3,000 a year could be gifted to any number of people without taxation (currently the amount is $10,000). Price's clients would give their children or grandchildren $3,000 and ask him to manage the money. But it was difficult for Price to manage so small a sum with adequate diversification of stocks. Ironically, Price started his first mutual fund as an accommodation to these clients. Managing a mutual fund, he could buy a diversified portfolio of stocks with the money represented by these gifts. Although he had been aware of mutual funds, Price had not been particularly interested in them.

The first U.S. mutual fund was started in Boston in 1924. U.S. funds were based on a 19th-century concept of investing that started in England. The idea was that a group of investors could pool their money, hire experienced money managers, and benefit from diversification as well as professional money management. Some of the English and Scottish trusts made investments in the form of loans or notes that helped finance the American economy—U.S. farm mortgages, railroads, and other industries—after the Civil War.

The original funds in England and Scotland were called trusts and were organized as closed-end funds. Unlike a mutual fund, a closed-end fund issues a fixed number of shares, which are usually traded on a stock exchange. Shares may trade above or below the actual value per share of the fund's net assets. Mutual funds are open-end investment companies that generally offer an unlimited number of shares and buy back shares based on the net asset value per share (net asset value is the value of the fund's investments plus other assets such as cash, minus all liabilities, divided by the number of shares outstanding).

Five years after the first U.S. fund opened, the 1929 stock market crash and the subsequent bear market halted the growth of funds. In 1936, the Securities and Exchange Commission worked with leaders of the mutual fund industry to draft rules and regulations. Their work produced the Investment Company Act of 1940, which set the structure and regulatory framework for the mutual fund industry.

When Price started his first fund in 1950, there were about 100 U.S. mutual funds. By the end of 1997, there were about 7,000.

Over the next ten years, the performance of Price's mutual fund skyrocketed. In 1960, Wiesenberger, A Thomson Financial Company that provides statistical and other services, reported that Price's growth fund had the best ten-year performance of any U.S. mutual fund—up almost 500 percent.

Price's Emerging Growth Fund and His Strategy to Protect Investments against Inflation

Price started his second fund in 1960. His objective for this fund was to buy stocks of smaller, emerging growth firms that had great potential for success. For a few years after its inception, the emerging growth fund did not perform well. In 1962, when the S&P 500 Index was off 9 percent, emerging growth stocks had a far worse correction and the fund dropped 29 percent. Clients complained and Price became disappointed and distraught. But he stayed with it, and performance improved. Five years later, the fund gained 44 percent; the S&P 500 increased only 9 percent. Price's investments in H&R Block, Xerox, Texas Instruments, and other firms became profitable as investors recognized their value and bought those stocks. By 1968, small growth stocks were so popular and money poured in so quickly that Price had to close the fund temporarily to protect shareholders. He didn't want to be under pressure to make investments when stock prices were at such high levels.

In a series of bulletins written for his firm in the late 1960s, Price said there would be "a new era for investors." He was concerned about the U.S. balance of international trade, high inflation and interest rates, and the low liquidity of financial institutions and many corporations.

"If a business recession occurs and unemployment increases materially, our social problems will become even more serious," Price warned. "Interest rates will have a bearing on earnings growth. If high rates of interest prevail (as would be expected during accelerated inflation), earnings per share may decline for companies that have to borrow money to provide for expansion and pay a rate of interest above the rate of return they receive on their invested capital."

Price correctly predicted that inflation and interest rates would climb and a major bear market would occur in future years. He started a third fund with the objective of protecting investments against inflation. For this fund, Price continued purchasing growth stocks, but the major change was that he bought stocks of natural resource–related firms owning or developing forest products, oil, and real estate. Price's plan was to adjust the number of natural resource stocks he held, depending on the level of inflation, interest rates, and the market climate. This strategy contradicted his buy-and-hold strategy for growth stocks. Analysts who worked for T. Rowe Price Associates disagreed and wanted to continue buying only growth stocks for the long term. Criticizing them, Price pointed out that investors must have the flexibility to change when conditions warrant change.

When gold was $35 an ounce in 1966, Price started buying. In 1975, the price of gold seemed high to many investors at $300 an ounce, but Price predicted that it would go a great deal higher. He was right. In 1980, gold reached a high of $850 an ounce.

Interest rates increased, stocks dropped sharply, and bonds became popular with investors. In 1967, three-month Treasury bills paid 4 percent; between 1973 and 1974, 8 percent; and between 1980 and 1981, the rate rose as high as 16 percent. Subsequently, interest rates began to fall and three-month Treasury bills paid about 6 percent by 1987.

Before the 1970s, Price and his colleagues bought some bonds for clients, but generally referred their clients to other reputable professionals who handled bonds. George Collins, a money manager specializing in bonds, was hired in 1971 to start a bond division for the firm. Collins purchased short-term bonds, Treasuries, and government agency obligations for the firm's clients, which allowed him to take advantage of the rise in interest rates. When the bonds and notes matured, with rates going up as they did, he could roll the money over and get higher yields. During this time, prices of stock funds dropped, but the bond portfolio produced excellent returns for clients.

In 1976, Collins created one of the first tax-free municipal bond funds. Tax-exempt bonds, issued by cities, states, and municipalities, had been around for a long time. The money raised by these bonds helps support government or local schools, airports, hospitals, roads, or highways. Interest paid on the bonds is generally exempt from federal income taxes. The reason there had been no tax-exempt bond funds was that prior to 1976, interest paid to shareholders of mutual funds was taxed as if it were taxable dividend income. Collins and others in the mutual fund industry were instrumental in getting Congress to change this. The Tax Reform Act of 1976 contained a provision allowing tax-exempt bond funds to pass through the tax-exempt interest in the form of tax-exempt dividends to shareholders.

T. Rowe Price Associates' first money market fund was started the same year. Money market funds are pools of assets invested in short-term debt obligations, usually maturing in less than a year. These funds are used as cash reserves for specific short-term needs and as a parking place for money until it can be invested. The main types of money market mutual funds are government money markets, general money markets, and tax-exempt money markets. Government money market funds own short-term government instruments such as Treasury bills. General money market funds may hold certificates of deposits, bank notes, short-term corporate debt, Treasury bills, and other short-term debt instruments. Tax-exempt money market funds own short-term debt obligations of municipalities, cities, and states. Although they are considered safe, money markets are not FDIC insured like bank accounts.

Today, T. Rowe Price Associates has a wide array of domestic, international, and global stock and bond mutual funds. Some of the firm's mutual funds are geared toward conservative investors for stability, income, and/or some growth, while others are appropriate for moderate or aggressive investors for greater growth.

Price's Legacy

Shaeffer succeeded Price as president. After Shaeffer retired, in 1974, other long-time associates ran the firm for the next decade. A new management team headed by George Collins took over in 1983, the year Price passed away. Although Price did not live to see his firm go public in 1986, he was amazed by the company's growth and content with what he had accomplished.

George A. Roche, current chairman and president of T. Rowe Price Associates, who worked with Price, says: "Price's philosophy was that the customer's interest should always come first and he wanted to be in the business of only managing money and providing related services. That was Price's original concept and that is how T. Rowe Price Associates is run. We manage accounts of individuals and institutions, mutual funds, and related business. Price's principles continue to be a very important part of our processes for investing. Procedures set up by Price and his original team of partners, Charlie Shaeffer and Walter Kidd, are still being followed. Price's emphasis on the importance of fundamental research, interviewing managers, and being alert to changes in the economy, industries, and firms is something we very much adhere to today."

PART V

John Templeton: The Spiritual Global Investor[1]

John Templeton, the Christopher Columbus of investors, ventured into emerging nations, explored their stock markets, and discovered profitable new worlds of investing. With the same type of determination as the great explorer, Templeton chartered a course that led him to acquire his fortune and become one of the greatest global money managers of our time.

Founder of the Templeton Mutual Fund Organization, he was one of the first U.S. money managers to invest internationally. Louis Rukeyser, host of television's *Wall $treet Week With Louis Rukeyser,* has referred to Templeton as "an authentic Wall Street hero." Don Phillips, CEO of Morningstar, has been inspired by Templeton: "John takes the long-term view, unlike many money managers who get hung up on the short term and become pessimistic. He has been an inspiration to me as an investor and also because of the great energy and spirit he brings to his activities." At about age 13, Phillips received a gift from his father of shares of Templeton's Mutual Fund, which led him to become interested in mutual funds.[2]

Templeton's well-thought-out reasons for buying stocks as well as his courage, foresight, and patience have paid off. Prior to World War II, the United States was in a recession. When the fighting began in Europe, Templeton felt that the war would create shortages of goods in the United States. Reasoning this would end the recession, he invested $10,000 and bought $100 worth of listed stocks selling at $1 a share or less. Four years later, Templeton sold his shares for over $40,000. In 1940, he went into business as a money manager, working with private clients.

In 1954, Templeton launched his first mutual fund, which invested worldwide. According to Lipper Analytical Services, this fund ranked number one in performance among its peers for 25 years, from 1967 to 1992. His business grew tremendously and he added many other funds that became successful.

In the 1960s and 1970s, Templeton was one of the first U.S. money managers to invest in Japan. He bought Japanese stocks as low as three times earnings and began selling when his stocks approached price-to-earnings ratios of 30. Known for recognizing stock buying opportunities before other investors and selling early, Templeton watched Japanese stocks continue to skyrocket after he sold. By this time, however, he felt Japan's stock market was overvalued and he was finding bargain-priced stocks in another part of the world—the United States. In fact, speaking to shareholders in 1988, Templeton said that the Japanese market might decline 50 percent or more. He was right. Within a few years, the Japanese stock market index, the Nikkei, fell more than 60 percent.

Argentinean stocks were severely depressed in 1985 due to very high inflation and political problems. Templeton saw this as an opportunity to buy stock bargains that he felt would recover from their low prices. Within four months, the International Monetary Fund (IMF) had negotiated a bailout for Argentina and Templeton's stocks had increased in value by 70 percent.

In 1997, speculation by investors, as well as severe political and economic problems in Asia, caused massive declines in Asian markets, somewhat reminiscent of the U.S. stock market crash of 1929. Templeton invested in South Korea and other parts of Asia. By 1999, some Asian markets had improved and Templeton had substantial profits. Descriptive of investing in Asia during this time is a quote from Templeton, "To buy when others are despondently selling and sell when others are avidly buying requires the greatest fortitude and pays the greatest potential reward."

Templeton's Spiritual Investments

To Templeton, moral and ethical values are an integral part of business and investing as well as life. John Galbraith, former chairman of Templeton Management Company, says that Templeton considers managing money "a sacred trust."

In 1992, Templeton sold the management companies of his mutual funds to Franklin Resources (Franklin Templeton Mutual Funds). "I stopped my business activities including investment management in order to devote my life to helping the spiritual growth of the world. My investments and those of my foundations are now mostly in mutual funds, which we think have wise management," Templeton says.

Encouraging spiritual and religious progress is not new to Templeton. In 1972, 20 years before he retired, Templeton established an annual prize for achievement in religion, which has been equated to a Nobel Prize, with awards of more than $1 million. Mother Teresa and the Reverend Billy Graham were among the early recipients. He established the John Templeton Foundation (templeton.org) in 1987 to support and encourage progress in religion by increasing spiritual information through scientific research. The foundation sponsors programs focusing on spiritual progress. Templeton created "The Honor Roll" for character building colleges in 1998. Many colleges and universities have taken the position that responsibility for character development and moral value judgment lies outside the realm of the academic world. Through "The Honor Roll," however, Templeton has chosen to recognize schools that strive to endow students with character as well as intellect, a sense of morality, and an ability to reason. The Laws of Life Essay Contest was established by Templeton for the purpose of awarding prizes to children in high school for writing 500–600 word essays on the most important spiritual values they have identified through their own personal experiences. In 1997, Templeton started the Templeton Foundation Press, which publishes inspirational and educational books written by him and other authors.

Among the many important, sensible spiritual principles Templeton espouses are:

- Thanksgiving [being thankful or grateful] results in more to be thankful for.

- You cannot be lonely while helping the lonely.
- You are only as good as your word.
- Enthusiasm is contagious.
- It is better to praise than to criticize.
- If you do not know what you want to achieve with your life you may not achieve much.[3]

Chapter 24

Templeton's Success Strategies: Foresight, Patience, and the Contrarian View

AT THE BEGINNING of his career, Templeton took a course in security analysis. His professor was Benjamin Graham. Like Graham, Templeton searched for stock bargains. As a young man, Templeton saved 50 cents out of every $1 he earned by shopping for the best bargains, whether it was for a home, car, clothes, furniture, or other items. Applying the concept of bargain hunting to purchasing stocks all over the world, Templeton equates his investment process to comparison shopping. Templeton also has used a contrarian investment strategy, buying when others are selling and the reverse.

Don Reed, president of Templeton Investment Counsel, describes an incident illustrating this strategy: "One day in the early 1990s when I was with John in New York, and Quaker Oats was very popular with investors, someone asked John why he didn't buy this stock. John replied, 'I eat the company's oat bran for breakfast every day and I know it is good for me—it keeps my cholesterol down. Quaker Oats is a fine company, but everybody knows it's a good firm and therefore is higher priced and not a bargain.'"[1]

Diversification is an especially important strategy when investing internationally. Owning a diversified portfolio of stocks can help to mitigate the potential impact of negative changes in currency values as well as political and economic risks. When Templeton was managing his mutual funds, he didn't have hard and fast rules for diversifying. Instead, he focused on finding the best stock values, and generally his portfolios were diversified as to companies, industries, and countries. Sometimes, however, he held a disproportionate number of stocks in Japan and the United States.

Have a Positive View and Be Prepared Emotionally and Financially for Bear Markets

"At the tender age of 85, Templeton renewed the lease on office space he rents for another ten years," says Mark Holowesko, illustrating Templeton's positive attitude.[2] Holowesko coordinates global equity research for the Franklin Templeton organization and also manages some mutual funds. A talented, bright money manager, he was hired and trained by Templeton, who became his mentor.

Templeton is also a realist. "Be prepared emotionally and financially for bear markets," cautions Templeton. "If you are really a long-term investor, you will view a bear market as an opportunity to make money."

Bubbles and Bursts

In 1991, during his annual meeting for shareholders, Templeton recommended that serious investors read the book by Charles Macay, *Extraordinary Popular Delusions and the Madness of Crowds*. Macay describes bubbles, which are periods of extreme speculation in stocks, bonds, real estate, collectibles, or other types of investments. A bubble can continue for months or even years. Ignoring fundamental values, investors buy on rumors or tips and are willing to pay almost any price. Eventually the value of the investments involved is recognized. Investors panic and widespread selling causes the bubbles to burst.

It is hard to believe, but one now-famous bubble occurred when people bought tulips in Holland. Imported from Turkey to Holland in 1600, tulips were at first displayed like works of art, and by 1634 had become a status symbol. Tulip prices began to increase and the flowers were even sold through stock exchanges. The public began speculating in tulips, driving prices higher and higher. Incredibly, people sold land, homes, and other possessions to buy tulips. The speculation ended when some tulip investors began to question the real value of these flowers. Investors started selling, fear turned into panic, fortunes were lost, and the tulip markets collapsed.

Other examples of bubbles include the U.S. stock market's advance between 1921 and 1929 (prior to the 1929 crash) and the Japanese stock market, which reached a high of about 39,000 in 1989 and fell to a low of 14,000 in 1992. Reflecting his sense of humor, Mark Holowesko has referred to some of the Internet stocks with earnings deficits that have sold at very high P/E ratios as "bubble.com."

Chapter 25

Templeton Applies the 3 Steps: Worldwide Comparison Shopping for Stocks

Step 1: Gather the Information

When Templeton was managing his mutual funds, to find leads and gather information, he read publications such as *The Wall Street Journal, Forbes,* and *Barron's.* He used Value Line research reports and studied company reports as well as industry publications.

Templeton worked with a team of analysts to identify undervalued stocks. Mark Holowesko uses the same approach. His investment selection process begins by searching databases of over 15,000 companies to find undervalued stocks and leads are generated through the fund group's worldwide research network. The analysts study financial reports and may travel to meet with the executives. Stocks considered the best values are kept on a list Holowesko refers to as "the bargain list," which is the basis of constructing his portfolios. The challenge of investing in undervalued stocks is to determine if a stock is cheap and should be, or if it is a real bargain in terms of future potential.

The Internet and electronic trading have made investing in many parts of the world easier, but there are obstacles, especially in emerging markets (markets of lesser-developed nations such as China). Different market trading systems, currencies, government policies, and accounting methods can make investing internationally difficult. The best way for individual investors lacking expertise in foreign markets to invest abroad is to buy mutual funds or hire money managers with good long-term track records for international investing. More experienced investors may want to buy American Depository Receipts (ADRs, covered later) listed on the New York Stock Exchange as well as mutual funds.

Morningstar and Value Line are two sources of information about mutual funds that invest worldwide. *Barron's* and *The Wall Street Journal* contain information that would be of help to investors of international stocks. Other sources for investing in global markets are newsletters such as John Dessauer's *Investors' World* (dessauerinvestorsworld. com) and *Emerging Markets Strategist,* published by the Bank Credit Analyst Research Group (bcapub.com). The New York Stock Exchange's Web site (nyse.com) contains the names of ADRs listed on the exchange.

Step 2: Evaluate the Information

To decide if a firm meets his criteria, Templeton would ask questions such as:

- Does the company have a strong management team?
- Is the company an industry leader?
- Does the company produce quality products and have well-established, entrenched markets?
- Does the company have a competitive advantage?
- Does the company have favorable profit margins and good return on shareholders' equity?
- Does the firm's balance sheet show good financial strength?
- Does the income statement show consistent sales and earnings growth?
- Is there a potential catalyst to increase share prices?
- Is the stock selling at a low price in relation to book value or current earnings and future probable earnings?

Prior to making investing decisions, Templeton studied financial reports of purchase candidates, comparing a company's financial

numbers with those of its competitors. He evaluated government policies that might impact the business. He looked for a catalyst that could
spark interest among investors, causing the company's stock price to
rise. A catalyst might occur when a company creates new markets,
products, or policies. Other catalysts could be potential mergers and
acquisitions and favorable change within an industry.

P/Es and Future Probable Earnings

Templeton would compare the current price-earnings ratio (the P/E is
covered in Step 2 of previous chapters for the other legends) of a stock
to the five-year average annual P/E. He compared P/Es from country
to country, and most importantly, he compared the price relative to his
estimate of probable earnings for the next five years. A stock with a
low P/E is not necessarily a bargain; it may turn out to be a loser
instead. In addition to low P/Es, Templeton looked for companies with
quality products, excellent employee relations, sound cost controls,
and the intelligent use of earnings by managers to grow their firms.

Templeton's Investments in Japan: Low P/Es and Future Potential Earnings

Today, Japan's stock market is one of the largest in the world in terms
of the combined value of all its stocks. When Templeton first invested
there in the 1960s and 1970s, Japan's total capitalization was worth
less than IBM's capitalization.

In 1949, Tokyo's stock market opened with the Nikkei Index at
179; about the same level as the Dow Jones Industrial Average that
year. In the years that followed, the Nikkei Index had a tremendous
rise and fall, reaching a high point of 39,000 in 1989. By 1992, the
bubble had burst and the Nikkei fell to a low of less than 14,000.
There had been excessive speculation in Japan's real estate market as
well as stocks.

At the time Templeton began investing in Japan, its stock market
was considered risky by investors who viewed Japan as a tiny country with low-quality goods. But what had transpired inside Japan led
to its great economic recovery.

Although World War II left Japanese factories in ruins and its
economy devastated, Japan's government, businesses, and labor united

to rebuild the country and develop the nation's industry and trade. After importing technology and raw materials from the West at a relatively low cost, Japan developed and exported products for the growing global market.

In 1992, during an interview for *Mutual Funds Update,* published by Wiesenberger, A Thompson Financial Company, Templeton commented: "Back in 1968, there were bargains in Japan that you just couldn't believe. We picked out the very finest, strong growth companies at three times earnings. That was so far out of line with America, where stocks were selling at 15 times earnings. We finally got up to 50 percent [of the mutual fund's assets] in Japan. That's as high as we ever got in any nation except in America."

In addition to the low P/Es, Templeton felt that the future earnings potential was excellent for the firms he bought. Among these companies were Hitachi, Nissan Motors, Matsushita Electric, Nippon Television, and Sumitomo Trust and Banking. Templeton got in on the ground floor before the Japanese stock market exploded on the upside.

Templeton also told *Mutual Funds Update,* "When stocks got up to 30 times earnings, we found bargains elsewhere, and in order to buy them we'd take profits, selling some of the Japanese stocks. But we got out much too soon (in 1986). There was such unreasonable optimism in Japan that they bid prices up to 75 times earnings. This was so high that we didn't own a single Japanese stock for over five years." In 1992, considering Japan's market was still overvalued for the most part, Templeton invested only in two Japanese stocks, Hitachi and Matsushita Electric.[1]

Profit Margins, Sales, and Future Prospects

Now part of Albertsons, American Stores was one of Templeton's largest holdings. Two companies, Skaggs and Acme, had merged and the resulting firm became American Stores. According to a history published by American Stores, both firms had been around a long time. Sam Skaggs opened his first store in 1915. Acme was started in 1891, when two retail pioneers opened several grocery stores. In 1979, L. S. Skaggs, CEO and grandson of Sam Skaggs, acquired Acme and adopted the name American Stores.

In 1986, Templeton discussed his purchase of American Stores with Phillip Harshram, a former senior editor for *Medical Economics Magazine,* during an interview for an article.[2] Templeton said that when Skaggs acquired Acme, it wasn't making much money and was selling at a low stock price: "We had every confidence that Skaggs, given a couple of years, could achieve the same profit margin with his merged companies that he'd come to expect from his original company. That was 2 percent, high for an industry that relies on volume. So we started buying it at $25 a share—getting $700 worth of sales volume with each share. Because 2 percent of $700 sales volume is $14 a share, we were buying American Stores for less than two times its potential per-share profit, and we bought more and more of it. The stock has since been split three for one, and the price on those split shares has risen to the $60 range, so our shares now are worth five or six times what we paid for them."

Harshram wrote in his article, "In the case of American Stores, the early tip-off to the stock's value came when Templeton spotted the high sales volume per share." The article quoted Templeton as saying: "It's not unlike making a medical diagnosis [Templeton's son, daughter, and daughter-in-law are physicians]. You have a hundred yardsticks, or symptoms, to consider and you can't afford to ignore any of them. But it doesn't take an experienced doctor long to know that only three or four are important to a given case, and he concentrates on them. The same is true of securities analysis. You deduce the basic values of a company from a particular set of measures, and you don't pay a lot of attention to measures that don't apply. In another company, you might look at a different set of measures—just as a doctor will look differently at the symptoms of each patient who comes in." In the case of American stores, Templeton looked at sales volume, previous profit margins, and management's potential for increasing profit margins as well as earnings. In the case of the other stocks, Templeton also used book value as a measure.

Buying Stocks below Book Value

During the late 1970s and early 1980s, U.S. auto companies faced severe problems. Oil prices were high and the public was buying small Japanese cars while U.S. auto companies were still producing large cars. Unions were demanding and getting higher wages. Due to the high level of pollution from car emissions, Congress passed a bill making it mandatory to have emission controls on cars, adding to the cost of production. Chrysler was in such bad shape the government had to bail the company out. Ford was losing money as well. Templeton decided to buy Ford.

After he bought Ford, the company reported additional losses. Investors continued selling, sending the price down further. Although he had a large position in Ford, Templeton was not overly concerned; he had bought the stock well below book value and didn't think Ford would go under. Templeton sold his shares later at about nine times his purchase price.

In the mid-1980s, Templeton purchased Australia and New Zealand Banking Group at a price of about $3.25 a share, selling well below book value.[3] On a comparative basis, U.S. bank stocks were selling at about 30 percent above book value per share and bank stocks in Japan were selling at 200 percent above book value per share.

A classic example of buying a bargain-priced stock under book value was Templeton's purchase of Japan's Yasuda Fire and Marine Insurance Company during the time he invested in Japan. Yasuda's selling price was 80 percent below the value of the firm's net liquid investments.[4]

Reminiscent of this purchase is a stock Mark Holowesko bought in 1998, Singapore Airlines. Holowesko bought Singapore Airlines below the cost of the aircraft per share. He was able to buy at such an inexpensive price because investors were negative about Asia during this time. *"Basically, stock prices in the short term tend to be moved by emotions. Longer term, they tend to reflect value,"* Holowesko says.

Step 3: Make the Decision

Before making his final buying decision, Templeton narrowed down his choices and compared them to each other. He wasn't just looking for a stock selling at a bargain price—Templeton was looking for the *best* bargain.

His average holding period for stocks has been about five years. Templeton might sell a stock that became overvalued based on his original buying criteria or if he were to find some negative information that would have precluded him from making the original purchase. According to Templeton, the best time for investors to sell is when they find a different stock worth 50 percent more than a current holding. This would include taxes and costs incurred upon the sale.

Chapter 26

Templeton's 15 Commonsense Rules for Investment Success

THE FOLLOWING ARE Templeton's 15 practical, timeless investment rules, written in his own words.[1]

1. Be Aware of the Real Return

"Invest for maximum total real return. This means return on invested dollars after taxes and inflation. This is the only rational objective for most long-term investors. Any investment strategy that fails to recognize the insidious effect of taxes and inflation fails to recognize the true nature of the investment environment and thus is severely handicapped. It is vital that you protect purchasing power."

[To illustrate the real return, suppose an investor bought a stock for $5,000, sold for $10,000, paid a capital gain of 20 percent, and inflation during the time was 1 percent. In this example, the real return would be $3,900.

  $5,000 gain
– 1,000 capital gain tax
  $4,000 after taxes
–   100 for inflation (loss of purchasing power of total capital–$10,000)
  $3,900 real return]

2. Invest, Don't Speculate

"Invest—don't trade or speculate. The stock market is not a casino, but if you move in and out of stocks every time they move a point or two, or if you continually sell short, or deal only in options, or trade in futures, the market will be your casino. And, like most gamblers, you may lose eventually—or frequently. You may find your profits consumed by commissions. You may find a market you expected to turn down turning up and up and up in defiance of all your careful calculations and short sales. Keep in mind the wise words of Lucien O. Hooper, a Wall Street legend: 'What always impresses me,' he wrote, 'is how much better the relaxed, long-term owners of stock are with their portfolios than the traders with their switching of inventory. The relaxed investor is usually better informed and more understanding of essential values, more patient and less emotional, pays smaller annual capital gains taxes, and does not incur unnecessary brokerage commissions.'"

3. Be Flexible

"Remain flexible and open-minded about different types of investments. There are times to buy blue-chip stocks, cyclical stocks, corporate bonds, convertible bonds, U.S. Treasury instruments, and other investments. And there are times to sit on cash, because sometimes cash enables you to take advantage of investment opportunities. The fact is there is no one kind of investment that is always best. If a particular industry or type of security becomes popular with investors, that popularity will prove temporary and when lost may not return for many years. Having said that, I should note, for most of the time, I have invested in common stocks because well-chosen stocks held for the long term have outperformed bonds and inflation in most decades with few exceptions, the most recent being the 1970s."

4. Buy Low: The Contrarian Approach

"Of course, you may say, buy low, that's obvious. Well it may be, but that isn't the way the market works. When prices are high, a lot of investors are buying. Prices are low when demand is low, investors have pulled back, people are discouraged and pessimistic. When almost everyone is pessimistic at the same time, the entire market collapses. Most often, just stocks in particular fields sustain losses. For example, industries such as automaking and casualty insurance go through regular cycles. Sometimes stocks of companies like the thrift institutions or money-center banks fall out of favor all at once. Whatever the reason, investors are on the sidelines, sitting on their wallets. Yes, they tell you: 'Buy low, sell high,' but all too many of them bought high and sold low. And when do they buy? The usual answer: 'Why, after analysts agree on a favorable outlook.' This is foolish, but it is human nature.

"It is extremely difficult to go against the crowd—to buy when everyone else is selling or has sold, to buy when things look darkest, to buy when so many experts are telling you that stocks in general, or in this particular industry, or even in this particular company, are risky right now. But, if you buy the same securities everyone else is buying, you will have the same results as everyone else. By definition, you can't outperform the market if you buy the market. And chances are if you buy what everyone is buying, you will do so only after it is already overpriced. Heed the words of the great pioneer of stock analysis Benjamin Graham: 'Buy when most people including experts are overly pessimistic, and sell when they are actively optimistic.'"

[One example is Templeton's early investment in Japan, discussed previously. In the late 1960s, when many American investors still thought of Japanese goods as inferior and thought Japan's stock market was not a good investment, Templeton did his homework, recognized value, and profited. Even though other investors disagreed with him, Templeton acted on his convictions backed up by his research. Another example is Templeton's purchase of Ford. When other investors were selling and Ford was reporting huge losses, Templeton saw a buying opportunity and profited.]

5. Buy Quality

"When buying stocks, search for bargains among quality stocks. Quality is a company strongly entrenched as the sales leader in a growing market. Quality is a company that's the technological leader in a field that depends on technical innovation. Quality is a strong management team with a proven track record. Quality is being the low-cost producer in an industry. Quality is a well-capitalized company that is among the first into a new market. Quality is a well-known, trusted brand for a high-profit-margin consumer product. Naturally, you cannot consider these attributes of quality in isolation. A company may be the low-cost producer, for example, but it is not a quality stock if its product line is falling out of favor with customers. Likewise, being the technological leader in a technological field means little without adequate capitalization for expansion and marketing.

"Determining the quality of a stock is like reviewing a restaurant. You don't expect it to be 100 percent perfect, but before it gets three or four stars you want it to be superior."

[Templeton bought quality companies dominant in their industries. Among Japanese stocks were Hitachi and Nissan Motors, and in the United States, American Stores (now part of Albertsons), Travelers (now part of Citigroup), and Ford Motors.]

6. Practice Value Investing

"Buy value, not market trends or the economic outlook. A wise investor knows that the stock market is really a market of stocks. While individual stocks may be pulled along momentarily by a strong bull market, ultimately it is the individual stocks that determine the market, not vice versa. All too many investors focus on the market trend or economic outlook. But individual stocks can rise in a bear market and fall in a bull market. The stock market and the economy do not always march in lockstep. Bear markets do not always coincide with recessions, and an overall decline in corporate earnings does not always cause a simultaneous decline in stock prices. So buy individual stocks, not the market trend or economic outlook."

7. Diversify

"Buy a number of stocks and bonds—there is safety in numbers. No matter how careful you are, no matter how much research you do, you can neither predict nor control the future. A hurricane or earthquake, an unexpected technological advance by a competitor, or a government-ordered product recall—any one of these can cost a company millions of dollars. Also, what looked like such a well-managed company may turn out to have serious internal problems that weren't apparent when you bought the stock. So you must diversify—by company, by industry, by risk, and by country. For example, if you search worldwide, you will find more bargains—and possibly better bargains—than in any single nation."

8. Do Your Homework

"Do your own research or hire wise experts to help you. Investigate before you invest. Study companies to learn what makes them successful. Remember, in most instances you are buying either earnings or assets, or both."

9. Monitor Your Investments

"Aggressively monitor your investments. Expect and react to change. No bull market is permanent. No bear market is permanent. And there are no stocks that you can buy and forget. The pace of change is too great. Remember, things change and no investment is forever."

10. Don't Panic

"Sometimes you won't have sold when everyone else is buying and you'll be caught in a market crash such as in 1987. There you are, facing a [large] loss in a single day.

"Don't rush to sell the next day. The time to sell is before the crash, not after. Instead, study your portfolio. If you didn't own these stocks now, would you buy them after the market crash? Chances are you would. So the only reason to sell them now is to buy other, more attractive stocks. If you can't find more attractive stocks, hold on to what you have."

[Based on Templeton's philosophy in the above scenario, before selling, investors should look at stock holdings in light of their buying criteria. Additionally, according to Templeton, the best time to sell is when an investor finds a stock worth 50 percent more than a current holding.]

11. Deal with Mistakes Effectively

"The only way to avoid mistakes is not to invest—which is the biggest mistake of all. So forgive yourself for your errors. Don't become discouraged and certainly don't try to recoup your losses by taking bigger risks. Instead, turn each mistake into a learning experience. Determine exactly what went wrong and how you can avoid the same mistake in the future. The big difference between those who are successful and those who are not, is that successful people learn from their mistakes and the mistakes of others."

[Investing mistakes, like other mistakes in life, are inevitable. Templeton has said that one-third of his investments do not work out; however, the rest—two-thirds of his investments—have brought him excellent profits. The important consideration is to acknowledge mistakes and, when possible, use them as a learning tool.]

12. Prayer Helps

"If you begin with a prayer, you can think more clearly and make fewer mistakes. [Templeton started his shareholders' meetings with a prayer. He believes in daily prayer and gratitude, but emphasizes that he doesn't pray for investment advice.] Prayer stills the mind and gives clarity of thought, which may help to make better decisions."

13. Be Humble

"An investor who has all the answers doesn't even understand all the questions. A know-it-all approach to investing will lead, probably sooner than later, to disappointment if not outright disaster. Even if you can identify an unchanging handful of investing principles, we cannot apply these rules to an unchanging universe of investments— or an unchanging economic and political environment. Everything is in a constant state of change and the wise investor recognizes that success is a process of continually seeing answers to new questions."

14. There's No Free Lunch

"This principle covers an endless list of admonitions. Never invest on sentiment. The company that gave you your first job or built the first car you ever owned, or sponsored a favorite television show of long ago, may be a fine company. But that doesn't mean its stock is a fine investment. Even if the corporation is truly excellent, prices of its shares may be too high. Never invest in an initial public offering (IPO) to save the commission [commissions are lower since he wrote this but are still a factor in the costs of investing]. That commission is built into the price of the stock—a reason why a great many new stocks decline in value after the offering. This does not mean you should never buy an IPO. But don't buy it to save the commission. Never invest solely on a tip. Why, that's obvious, you might say. It is. But you would be surprised how many investors, people who are well educated and successful, do exactly this. Unfortunately, there is something psychologically compelling about a tip. Its very nature suggests inside information, a way to turn a fast profit."

15. Have a Positive Attitude toward Investing

"Do not be fearful or negative too often. For 100 years optimists have carried the day in U.S. stocks. Even in the dark 1970s, many professional money managers and many individual investors made money in stocks, especially those of smaller companies. There will, of course, be corrections, perhaps even crashes. But, over time, our studies indicate stocks do go up and up and up. As national economies become more integrated and interdependent, as communication becomes easier and cheaper, business is likely to boom. Trade and travel will continue to grow. Wealth will increase and stock prices should rise accordingly. The financial future is bright and the basic rules of building wealth by investing in stocks hold true . . . it's still buy low, sell high."

Chapter 27

The Evolution and Importance of Global Investing

SINCE THE TIME Templeton began his investment career, there has been a tremendous surge in global trade and investing. Nations outside the United States have expanded their economies, and their stock markets have grown. In 1970, U.S. markets represented 66 percent of the world's stock markets (based on capitalization). In 1997, U.S market share compared with other world markets was about 40 percent.

The collapse of the Berlin Wall in 1989 and the fall of communism in the former Soviet Union and Eastern Europe created new and unprecedented opportunities for increased international trade. Economic reforms and privatization of state-run telephone and electric companies, banks, and other businesses in Latin America and Asia have fostered free enterprise. The opening of China to the global economy has added over a billion potential customers and expanded opportunities for China as well as other nations.

In January 1999, the euro began trading. The euro was created to help make members of the European Common Monetary Union (EMU) more competitive and trade between nations easier. Plans called for the initial members to include Austria, Belgium, Finland, France, Germany, Ireland, Italy, Luxembourg, the Netherlands, Portugal, and Spain, with the United Kingdom and others joining later. The goal of the EMU has been to make companies more efficient and profitable by creating more uniform accounting systems, common monetary policies, and a common currency.

Global Diversification

Some investors question the need to own foreign stocks in order to earn profits from abroad. Their rationale is that because many U.S. companies, such as McDonald's, Coca-Cola, Disney, and IBM, rely on foreign operations for significant portions of their income, investors only need to own domestic firms with market share abroad in order to benefit from worldwide earnings and potential stock profits.

Templeton believes that investors who only buy U.S. stocks are limiting potential to earn greater returns by excluding some of the world's top-producing companies. In addition, investment returns of some foreign markets have been higher than U.S. returns. In the short term, world stock markets sometimes appear to move in sync, but over the longer term, global markets have performed differently. One country's stock market may advance while another's declines. Owning well-selected stocks in different companies, industries, and countries can reduce risk, as illustrated in the next chart, Best Performing Foreign Markets versus the United States.

Best Performing Foreign Stock Markets versus the United States

Year	Foreign Market Performance*		United States Market Performance**
1987	Japan	+ 43.2	+3.91
1988	Belgium	+ 55.4	+15.91
1989	Austria	+104.8	+31.36
1990	United Kingdom	+ 10.3	−2.08
1991	Hong Kong	+ 49.5	+31.33
1992	Hong Kong	+ 32.3	+ 7.36
1993	Hong Kong	+116.7	+10.07
1994	Finland	+ 52.5	+2.00
1995	Switzerland	+ 45.0	+38.19
1996	Spain	+ 41.3	+24.05
1997	Portugal	+ 43.9	+34.09
1998	Finland	+122.6	+30.72

* Morgan Stanley Capital International, in U.S. dollars with gross dividends
**Morgan Stanley Capital International, in U.S. dollars with gross dividends, percentage change yearly

Categories of Global Markets

The terms *global* and *international* are sometimes used interchangeably, but they have different meanings. International investors buy stocks or bonds outside their country. Global investors have no geographic boundaries; they can invest anywhere. Global stock and bond markets are categorized as developed or emerging. Developed nations consist of countries with established, mature economies, such as the United States, Canada, France, Germany, Italy, the United Kingdom, Sweden, Switzerland, Finland, Norway, the Netherlands, Austria, New Zealand, and Japan.

An emerging nation is generally defined as a country in the developmental stage of economic growth. Stock markets of these nations are usually small and have more risk than those of developed nations. Emerging markets include China, Russia, India, Indonesia, Brazil, Mexico, Turkey, Thailand, Iran, Egypt, Korea, Poland, South Africa, Colombia, Argentina, Peru, and Venezuela. As they grow and become more stable, emerging markets can be classified as developed markets.

The Challenges of Global Investing

Investors of foreign stocks may face difficulties due to differences in government policies, changing currency rates, and accounting standards. Additionally, the same risks incurred domestically—increasing interest and inflation rates, economic recessions, and general market declines—can affect foreign stock markets.

Currency Rates

U.S. travelers who exchange dollars for other currencies when traveling abroad may realize a loss when converting the local currency back into dollars if the dollar goes down in value. Conversely, they may have a profit if the dollar rises when they convert back into dollars. When U.S. investors of foreign securities sell stocks, they also could have gains or losses due to fluctuations in exchange rates. Factors that play a role in the value of a country's currency rates include political and economic conditions and inflation and interest rates.

Experienced investors or investment professionals may use hedging techniques to offset the possibility of the currency risk. Although hedging is not recommended for the average investor, it is useful to have a general understanding of it. If investors using hedging techniques expect the dollar to strengthen, they lock in a currency-exchange rate to protect the portfolio against a decline in the dollar value of their foreign holdings. This can be accomplished by buying a foreign currency futures contract, an investment technique that uses a preset exchange rate for buying U.S. dollars. On the other hand, investors who expect the U.S. dollar to weaken leave foreign holdings unhedged with the potential of benefiting from increases in the value of the foreign currency. A hedging strategy can be risky, however, because the investor may not be correct about the direction of the U.S. dollar.

Templeton used a different approach. For the most part, Templeton owned diversified portfolios of stocks in different countries and currencies and he left his portfolio unhedged. This policy reduces risk because currencies don't move in unison.

Opportunities and Risks of Emerging Markets

Investing in emerging markets is not a new concept. In 1873, one of the first investments made by a newly formed Scottish investment company, SAINTS, was in an emerging nation—the United States. During that time, the United States was still overcoming the devastation of the Civil War and its future was uncertain.

Investors who buy stocks of emerging markets have an opportunity for huge profits, but they also face the potential danger of large losses. Generally, these markets have high volatility and can go up and down in a seesaw-like fashion. For instance, Turkey's stock market was up 85 percent in 1997 and fell 51 percent in 1998 (illustrated in the chart Volatility of Emerging Markets).

Emerging markets can have extremely low or even no trading volume at times, making it difficult to buy or sell. Government supervision is sometimes lax and full disclosure of information can be a problem. Investors of emerging markets may see their stocks decline due to political and economic problems. In 1994, Mexico devalued the peso and its stock market tumbled as a result. Subsequently, the United

Volatility of Emerging Markets

Year	Best			Worst	
1988	Brazil	126%		Portugal	− 28%
	Korea	113		Greece	− 38
	Mexico	108		Turkey	− 61
1989	Turkey	503		Colombia	− 12
	Argentina	176		Korea	− 7
	Thailand	101		Venezuela	− 33
1990	Venezuela	602		Taiwan	− 51
	Greece	104		Philippines	− 54
	Chile	40		Brazil	− 66
1991	Argentina	307		Colombia	− 12
	Colombia	191		Turkey	− 42
	Mexico	107		Indonesia	− 42
1992	Thailand	40		Greece	− 19
	Colombia	39		Venezuela	− 42
	Malaysia	28		Turkey	− 42
1993	Poland	970		Venezuela	− 11
	Turkey	214		Nigeria	− 18
	Philippines	132		Jamaica	− 57
1994	Brazil	65		Poland	− 43
	Peru	48		Turkey	− 43
	Chile	42		China	− 49
1995	Jordan	23		Pakistan	− 34
	South Africa	15		India	− 35
	Peru	11		Sri Lanka	− 40
1996	Russia	143		South Africa	− 17
	Hungary	133		Korea	− 33
	Venezuela	101		Thailand	− 36
1997	Russia	98		Thailand	− 76
	Turkey	86		Indonesia	− 72
	Hungary	54		Korea	− 70
1998	Korea	99		Russia	− 85
	Greece	87		Turkey	− 51
	Costa Rica	86		Venezuela	− 51

Source: Emerging Market Strategist, published by the Bank Credit Analyst Research Group

States along with the International Monetary Fund (IMF) bailed out the Mexican government. Mexico's problems paled, however, in comparison with the economic and currency crises of Asia in 1997. In fact, the Mexican stock market gained about 55 percent in 1997.

Fueled by an influx of money from European and U.S. investors, Asian nations had experienced rapid growth for over a decade. In 1996, the gross domestic product (GDP) of Malaysia increased 8.4 percent; Thailand, 6.7 percent; and Indonesia, 7.8 percent compared with 2.4 percent in the United States (and in 1999, about 4 percent). But Asian growth was financed with massive debt based on unsound business and economic policies. There was a tremendous overbuilding of factories and manufacturing plants leading to overcapacity. Excessive speculation in building and real estate caused many banks to be overextended with nonperforming loans. Stock markets became overheated and exports slowed.

In 1997, news of plummeting Asian currencies and stock markets made headlines. Unwise lending policies and lack of government supervision culminated in bank failures in Thailand, Malaysia, Indonesia, Philippines, and South Korea. Thailand devalued its currency, the baht, in July 1997. Devaluations of Malaysia's ringgit and Indonesia's rupiah followed, and South Korea's won dropped sharply. Highly leveraged businesses with little equity were restructured or went bankrupt. Conflicts of interest and inept business policies were contributing factors.

The IMF committed billions of dollars to bail out these countries. Established in 1945 to stabilize global markets, the IMF now has over 181 member nations. Member nations contribute funds based on assigned quotas in relation to their financial strength. When the IMF lends money to nations in financial trouble, it expects them to cut their budget deficits, raise interest rates, or take other necessary actions. The IMF required South Korea to relax restrictions and allow some foreigners to take over failing banks. Although the IMF came under criticism for policies that were considered too burdensome, South Korea's economy has since improved, as well as those of other nations in Asia.

At the end of 1997 the stock market of Thailand was off 76.75 percent; Malaysia, 68.13 percent; South Korea 66.67 percent; Indonesia 73.92 percent; and the Philippines, 60.30 percent.

Political and economic crises cause losses and pain, but if sound monetary and business policies are instituted the result can be renewed growth and stronger economies. These crises can also create buying opportunities for investors who take a long-term view. For example, South Korea's market, where Templeton invested in 1997, was up over 141.5 percent in 1998 and 92.4 percent in 1999 (according to statistics of Morgan Stanley Capital International, reflecting reinvested dividends).

Don Reed, president of Templeton Investment Council comments, "During crises such as these in Asia, stocks that appear attractive may not be bargains. Companies exporting goods, for instance, might be obvious purchase candidates because they have a competitive advantage; currency devaluation makes products of exporters less expensive. But, it is important to select companies generating sufficient cash and not dependent on borrowing because credit is generally very tight. We recast financial statements of purchase candidates to reflect currency devaluations."

Chapter 28

Applying Templeton's Strategies for Different Types of Investors

TEMPLETON WOULD ADVISE conservative investors to invest worldwide by purchasing mutual or closed-end funds. Mutual funds are defined as open-end funds because they constantly issue and redeem shares. Closed-end funds have a fixed number of shares and trade publicly like stocks. Closed-end funds can sell at a premium or a discount to net asset value, which is the value of the underlying investments divided by the number of shares outstanding. Mutual funds sell at net asset value plus a commission, if there is a commission charge (there may be a surrender charge). Additionally, conservative investors can hire a money manager who invests worldwide.

A Variety of Choices among Global and International Funds Investing Worldwide

Global or international funds offer a diversified portfolio of professionally managed stocks. International funds limit investments to foreign stocks. Global funds can invest anywhere. There are funds that invest in a single country and regional funds that limit their investment to a specific geographic region such as Europe, the Pacific, or Latin America. Some funds concentrate on developed nations like the United

States, Japan, England, Germany, and France. Others limit stock purchases to emerging nations such as China, Korea, Turkey, the Czech Republic, India, and Russia. Funds that invest in emerging markets, single country funds, and regional funds are usually more risky. Although conservative investors might own some of these funds, generally they would be more suitable for moderate or aggressive investors. It is also advisable to diversify among funds or money managers.

Prior to investing, questions to ask money managers of mutual funds and closed-end funds, or private money managers include:

- What is the experience of the prospective manager in international investing?
- What is the fund's track record for at least five years?
- What is the manager's investment method, philosophy, and criteria?
- Will the manager be investing in emerging or developed markets, or both?

Moderate or aggressive investors can buy stocks on a foreign stock exchange, but drawbacks may include language barriers, trading restrictions, and low trading volume. Investors who buy stocks of a foreign country should have an understanding of the nation's accounting system because methods of accounting vary among nations. Buying on foreign stock exchanges is suggested only for very experienced investors.

American Depository Receipts

Foreign stocks can also be bought in the form of American Depository Receipts (ADRs). Generally issued by U.S. banks that have branches overseas, ADRs are negotiable certificates representing ownership of shares in a foreign company traded on a foreign exchange. The bank usually charges a fee and provides periodic as well as annual reports, and year-end tax information. Examples of stocks traded as ADRs are Royal Dutch Petroleum, Sony, and SmithKline Beecham.

An advantage for U.S. investors buying ADRs listed on a U.S. stock exchange such as the New York or American stock exchanges is that companies represented by the ADRs are required by the Securities and Exchange Commission to conform to U.S. accounting standards. Before investing in ADRs, however, it is advisable to have experience investing in domestic stocks as well as some knowledge of foreign markets. To mitigate the risks of international investing, buy several different ADRs of financially strong firms and also consider buying funds for additional diversification.

Chapter 29

Templeton's Positive View: The Future of Free Enterprise and the Stock Market

AN INVESTOR'S ATTITUDE can affect his or her success in investing as well as other areas of life. Templeton has a positive view of the future of free enterprise and the stock market. He made the following comments during a talk he gave to the Empire Club of Canada in May 1995.[1]

"Today corporations are being created at the rate of 4,000 every business day. Underlying this growth is the increasing acceptance of free trade and enterprise within and among nations. Global restructuring is expected to bring four billion new people into the free-market system. The trend toward greater capitalism and freedom unleashes tremendous potential for efficiency gains and even greater wealth potential.

"Technology has changed life. Only 50 years ago, there were no photocopiers, lasers, microchips, satellites in space, fax machines, e-mail, computers, Internet or online data services, videocassette recorders or cellular phones. There have also been substantial educational advances. When I was born in 1912, there were two graduate schools of business in the world. Today, there are more than 600 in North America alone. The level of education is improving around the world. For example, in China, the literacy rate has increased from less than 20 percent in 1950 to more than 60 percent today. Progress has been tremendous in the field of medicine. Death from tuberculosis, pneumonia, diabetes, and many other diseases that were once considered fatal is now only a tiny fraction of what it was 50 years ago. Work in biotechnology and other new areas of medical science offers hope for treatment of multiple sclerosis, arthritis, and AIDS."

Templeton considers the spiritual aspect of life more important than all the other aspects combined. "There is so much that remains to be discovered in this aspect of our lives." He explains: "Much more can be accomplished if we work toward spending at least one-tenth on spiritual research as on material research. New beneficial concepts can develop. Religion can have an unlimited impact on our attitudes, goals, motivations, and interrelations with others. While there are many problems, if one focuses on the bigger picture there are numerous reasons to be thankful for living in a time of remarkable progress and wonderful possibilities for the future."

Templeton's Outlook for the Stock Market and Spiritual Progress

During the third annual Institutional Investment Management Summit presented by Frank J. Fabozzi, November 18, 1999, Templeton was a guest speaker at a special luncheon. He was the recipient of the Consulting Group's (a division of Salomon Smith Barney) inaugural "Pioneers of Investing" award.

Looking physically fit and remarkably young at age 87, Templeton started his speech with what seemed like a startling prediction. He said that the Dow Jones Industrial Average will be over 1,000,000 by the end of the 21st century, adding that his predictions are not always correct. Templeton's prediction may sound high. However, early in the 20th century the Dow was about 100 (the Dow was actually lower at the very beginning of the century, but he was using ballpark numbers). Because the Dow was around 10,600 the day of Templeton's speech, it had increased approximately 100 times. If the Dow increases by the same amount, based on a starting level of 10,000, in the 21st century it will be over 1,000,000.

Inspired by Templeton's speech, Michael Dieschbourg and Mark Kennard of the Consulting Group projected when the Dow could cross the 1,000,000 at different annualized returns (this does not include dividends):

Annualized Return (Percentage)	Year the Dow Reaches 1,000,000
10.0	2047
7.5	2062
5.3	2087
4.6	2099

Of course, a severe bear market could change the course of the Dow Jones and the Index may perform better or worse in the 21st century than in the 20th. Templeton also warned, "Be prepared for bear markets [which may last for longer periods of time than in recent years]." Bear market declines and recovery cycles are illustrated in the charts that follow.

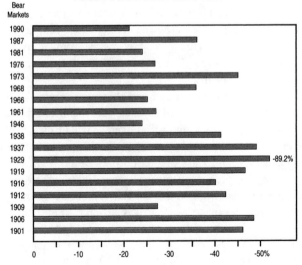

Bear Market Declines
Percent Decline from Peak to Bottom

Source: InvesTech Research

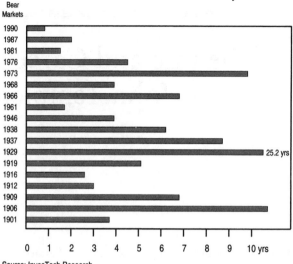

Bear Market Recovery Cycles
Time from Market Peak to 100% Recovery

Source: InvesTech Research

Addressing this audience of pension plan sponsors, investment managers, and investment consultants, he went on to talk about spiritual matters: "The difference between love and money is that when one has a fixed amount of money and gives a part of it away, there is less money. But when one gives away love, the reverse is true—there is more love." He also said that spiritual information could increase 100 times in the 21st century, leaving many in the crowd thinking about spiritual wealth as well as material wealth as they exited the room for their next meeting.

Chapter 30

The Life and Career of John Templeton

TEMPLETON WAS BORN in 1912 in the small town of Winchester, Tennessee. His parents, Harvey and Vella, were extraordinary people. Harvey, an industrious, innovative man, was a farmer, built homes, and worked at other jobs. Vella, a talented, bright, and deeply religious woman, inspired John to have faith in God and confidence in himself. The qualities Templeton learned from his parents—integrity, charity, enthusiasm, discipline, confidence, and humility—prepared him to overcome the adversities and challenges of life. He also gained the ability to see the positive aspects of life in a world seemingly filled with negatives.[1]

Templeton's School Years and Career

In school, Templeton studied the lives of the industrialists. He read about Benjamin Franklin, who said, "Money begets money and its offspring begets more." Fascinated with how money could grow, Templeton spent hours playing with compound interest tables. He was still talking about the wonder of compound interest years later.

In 1991, speaking to shareholders of his funds, Templeton said, "If the Native Americans who sold Manhattan Island to the Dutch in 1626 for the equivalent of $24 invested the money at 8 percent, the compounding would have produced enough cash today to buy back all the real estate now on Manhattan Island and there would be billions of dollars left over." His advice to investors is: "Become educated about investments—learn about the risks and rewards—start investing as early in life as possible to take advantage of the power of compound interest."

"John made up his mind when he was age 11 that he was going to be wealthy," according to Harvey Templeton Jr., his brother.[2]

Upon completing high school, Templeton received a scholarship to Yale. When he was a sophomore there in 1931, he became interested in the stock market. Noticing the wide fluctuations of stock prices, he reasoned that one company's business value couldn't fluctuate that much in the space of a year.

Templeton explained: "I decided that what I could do well was to judge the values of corporations and advise people when the price of a share was too low or too high in relation to the true value of the company. So I majored in economics at Yale and graduated second in my class and, as a result, got a Rhodes scholarship. And although I was studying for my degree at Oxford, in law, I was really preparing myself to be an investment counselor, particularly by studying foreign nations. In two years and seven months, I traveled through 35 countries [in Europe and Japan], always trying to learn as much as I could that would be useful in the future to judge the values of corporations on a worldwide basis. My concept was that you can't tell the value of a corporation if you study only one nation; many products are in competition worldwide. You have to know the whole industry worldwide before you can make proper estimates of the earnings power in the future."[3]

After completing his law degree at Oxford, Templeton returned to the United States and got a job in the newly formed investment counsel division of a stock brokerage firm. In 1940, he opened his own business as an investment counselor. At first, he worked with private clients, but in 1954 he started his first global fund and subsequently created other successful funds.

Templeton's Spiritual Investments

Templeton's long-term investment goal was not to achieve a fortune for the sake of having wealth in and of itself, but rather to help others and promote causes related to spiritual development. Even when he became a money manager, he also thought about managing money from the perspective of helping others make money.

Templeton believes that progress begins with inquiry and he has devoted his life to what he calls "humility theology." In his book, *The Humble Approach,* Templeton says: "Humility is the gateway to understanding. As thanksgiving opens the door to spiritual growth, so does humility open the door to progress in knowledge and also to progress in theology. Humility is the beginning of progress. Humility leads to open-mindedness. It is difficult for a person to learn anything more if he [or she] knows it all already. When we realize how little we know, we can begin to seek and to learn."[4]

Templeton was knighted by Queen Elizabeth in 1987 for his service in philanthropy. One of his greatest philanthropic works is the Templeton Prize. Established by him in 1972, it has been equated to a Nobel Prize for achievement in religion. Mother Teresa, the Reverend Billy Graham, and Alexander Solzhenitsyn have been among the recipients.

"This award is given to a person who has made an original contribution resulting in a great increase in either humankind's love or understanding of God," according to Templeton. The annual prize of over $1 million is intended to bring awareness to the fact that resources and manpower are needed for progress in spiritual knowledge, and to encourage the creation of more contributions to works in this area.

In 1987, Templeton established a foundation to support and encourage progress in religion by increasing spiritual information through scientific research. Templeton's son John Jr., a doctor, left his successful surgical practice to serve full time as president. Among the members of the board of advisors are Dr. Herbert Benson, president of the Mind/Body Medical Institute; Lawrence Rockefeller, business executive and philanthropist; and Nobel Laureate, Sir John Eccles. The board also consists of theologians from different religions.

Charles Johnson, CEO of Franklin Resources, says, "Sir John Templeton, who is one of the most brilliant investors, has proven his value both in the field of investments and in philanthropy, and set a high standard for the financial world. John is truly a treasure of our time."[5]

PART VI

Creating
Your Own
Wealth Plan

How You Can Apply a Composite Version of the 3 Steps and Project Potential Investment Returns

NOW THAT YOU have read how the legends invest, this chapter focuses on how you can apply a composite version of the 3 Steps. Additionally, there is an explanation of a method to project a company's future earnings, stock price, and your potential investment return.

Step 1: Gather the Information

Like the legends, you can find investment leads and gather information in a variety of ways: reading business publications such as *The Wall Street Journal, The New York Times, Forbes, Fortune, USA Today, Barron's,* and *Financial World;* finding outstanding products while shopping in stores or on the Internet; talking with business and investment professionals.

Price read various publications to find leads and gather information, clipping items of interest, which he referred to later. Fisher has talked with business people and investment professionals to get leads. Buffett has found products he likes, has become a customer of the company, and later has bought the stock or even the whole firm.

Once you have identified purchase candidates, study company reports (the annual, 10-K, 10-Q, and 8-K reports, and the proxy statement) as well as those of industry competitors. Company reports can be obtained by visiting a firm's Web site or calling or e-mailing their investor relations departments. You can also visit the Security and Exchange Commission's Web site (www.sec.gov) or EDGAR Data Service (freeedgar.com). Names of competitors can be found through stock research services and might be provided by a company's investor relations department.

A tremendous volume of information is available for researching companies with computer software products and on the Internet. The following is a composite list of various categories of Web sites and companies that sell computer software for screening stocks (covered in previous chapters) and some additional Web sites:

Stock Research

- Value Line (valueline.com)
- Bloomberg Financial (www.bloomberg.com)
- Standard & Poor's (www.standardandpoor.com)
- Morningstar (morningstar.com)
- Market Guide (marketguide.com)
- Yahoo! (yahoo.com)
- MoneyCentral (moneycentral.msn.com/investor)
- Investorama (investorama.com)
- Inve$tWare (investware.com)

Background Information about Companies and Corporate Executives

- Infotrac (www.galegroup.com) and other databases for research articles
- Hoover's Inc. (hoovers.com) for company profiles
- *The Wall Street Journal*'s Interactive Edition (wsj.com) (see link to company briefing book)
- Best Calls (bestcalls.com) for information about conference calls

Information about Insider Buying

- MoneyCentral (moneycentral.msn.com/investor)
- Insider Trader (insidertrader.com)
- Thomson Investor Network (www.thomsoninvest.net)

Estimates of Future (Projected) Earnings for Many Companies

- Zacks (zacks.com)
- Value Line (valueline.com)
- Market Guide (marketguide.com)

Information about Mutual Funds That Invest Worldwide

- Morningstar (morningstar.com)
- Value Line (valueline.com)

Newsletters Covering Global Investments

- John Dessauer's *Investors' World* (dessauerinvestorsworld.com)
- Emerging Markets Strategist (bcapub.com)

American Depository Receipts (ADRs) Listed on the New York Stock Exchange

- The New York Stock Exchange (nyse.com)

Economic Statistics

- The Conference Board (www.conference-board.org)
- The Department of Labor's Bureau of Labor Statistics (stats.bls.gov) for labor statistics and inflation rates

Firms That Forecast Consumer and Business Trends

- Kiplinger Reports (kiplinger.com)
- H.S. Dent Forecast Newsletter (www.hsdent.com)

Companies That Sell Computer Software Programs for Screening Stocks

- Value Line (valueline.com)
- Standard & Poor's (standardandpoor.com)
- Morningstar (morningstar.com)
- American Association of Individual Investors (aaii.com)
- National Association of Investors Corporation (better-investing. org)

Step 2: Evaluate the Information

Comparing evaluating a stock to reviewing a restaurant, Templeton says, "You don't expect it to be 100 percent perfect, but before it gets three or four stars, you want it to be superior."

Here is a composite version of questions the legends might ask to determine if a stock meets their criteria, followed by sources of information to help you find the answers. For the first set of questions, you may want to review Chapters 2 and 3.

Getting to Know the Company and Its Management

- Is the business understandable?
- What are the goals of the business and the plan to achieve them?
- What are the risks of the business?
- Does management report to shareholders candidly?
- Is the company repurchasing its shares?
- Do the top executives own a significant amount of the company's stock?
- Are insiders buying a significant amount of the company's stock?

Corporate executives discuss the goals and risks of their businesses in annual reports. They may also describe their policies for buying back their shares in company reports.

To answer the question of whether a company is reporting candidly, read management's comments about the firm's goals, sales, earnings, and other performance numbers in company reports for the past five (or more) years. Then compare the comments with the actual results. Look at how executives report in bad times as well as good. Put words like "we have built shareholder value" in perspective with the actual performance numbers. In his book, *How to Profit from Annual Reports*,[1] Richard Loth mentioned an annual report that said, "the past year was truly one of accomplishments," but these words were followed by a lengthy discussion of what went wrong because company sales were down, operating earnings were off, and net income per share fell by 50 percent.

If the top executives of a company own a substantial amount of stock in their business, they tend to think and act in alignment with shareholders' interests. The proxy statement lists the compensation and amount of shares held by corporate executives.

Some investors, such as John Spears, look for companies with substantial insider buying (purchases by officers, executives, and other employees) that meet additional criteria as well. Jonathan Moreland, director of research at Insider Trader defines substantial insider buying as, "An investment by more than one insider (preferably several insiders) totaling at least $50,000 for smaller companies and at least $100,000 for larger firms." Moreland also emphasizes, "Insiders can be wrong."

Putting Management, Policies, and Products under a Microscope

- Does the company have an outstanding CEO and a strong management team?
- Do the executives have a track record of innovative policies and products?
- Does the firm maintain excellent customer, employee, and executive relations?
- Does the company have top-quality products that command high customer loyalty?

Questions like the ones above relative to the quality of management are more subjective. But if you are going to use a buy-and-hold strategy, it is advisable to find out as much as possible about the firm's top executives. Mason Hawkins thinks of buying a stock as if he were becoming a partner with management.

Fisher seeks answers to these type of questions by getting the "scuttlebutt." He talks with customers, suppliers, competitors, and others related to the company (see Chapter 14). After Fisher completes his background research, he meets with the top executives of a company to ask further questions relevant to their business. He may ask them about future plans for R&D, expenses and cost controls, potential or current competitive problems, and questionable items on financial statements.

Fisher's scuttlebutt method is best suited for enterprising investors who are investigating small, local firms and not practical for many investors. But there are alternative methods of getting background information, as discussed in Chapter 16. A company's Web site is a good place to start. In addition to general information about the company and shareholders' reports, you may find recordings or transcripts of conference calls (typically conducted by the CFO or president) and speeches or interviews given by the CEO at the Web site.

Using the Internet or a database like Infotrac, search for current and past articles about the company and its top executives in business publications, industry trade journals, and stock research reports. At the same time, you can also research the competition.

After completing background research, if possible, meet the firm's top executives or contact them by phone and ask pertinent questions. If this is not possible, you can talk with a representative of the company's investor relations department. Be aware that the level of knowledge of people in investor relations departments varies from company to company. If you can't get your questions answered by the representative, ask to speak with the head of the investor relations department.

You may already be familiar with the company's products and have the ability to compare them with the competitors' products. This works best with companies selling consumer products. More research may be required for other types of companies. One way to get competitors' opinions of your purchase candidate is to contact executives or investor relations departments of several competing firms. Ask them how the company you are considering compares with their firm.

Company reports often discuss policies for attracting and retaining employees and may have information about employee benefits and employee training.

Examining the Company's Financial Numbers

- Does the company have a wide competitive advantage?
- Is the business generating good free cash flows (owner earnings)?
- Does the business have a long-term history of increasing sales and earnings at a favorable rate of growth?

- Has the company achieved a good return on shareholders' equity compared with its competitors' returns and alternative investments?
- Has the company maintained favorable profit margins compared with its competitors' profit margins?
- Is the company's debt reasonable?
- Does the company have an uninterrupted long-term record of paying dividends?

Financial numbers and ratios—sales and earnings, free cash flows, profit margins, return on shareholders' equity, debt, and dividends—can be found in company reports and through stock research services in print or online. To determine if a business has a wide competitive edge, compare the company with its competitors regarding the financial track record, quality of management and products (or services), and distribution capability of products (or services) in domestic and international markets.

Determine If the Stock Price Is Attractive

Is the stock selling at an attractive price relative to:

- Sales per share?
- Book value per share?
- Current P/E?
- Future potential earnings per share in five or ten years?
- Future potential stock price?

Stock research services (previously mentioned in Step 1) provide ratios to help determine whether the price of a stock is attractive. These ratios can be calculated from numbers found in company reports as well (you may also want to review Chapters 3, 7, and 16).

Market Guide, MoneyCentral, and other stock research services have stock ratio comparisons—for example, a stock's current P/E compared with the five-year high and low P/E and the P/E of an index such as the Standard & Poor's 500 (see Chapter 9). Zacks has securities analysts' estimates of future earnings. Value Line provides projections of earnings and future potential stock prices. You can also attempt to project a company's future earnings and potential stock price (see the example at the end of this chapter).

All this research may seem like a lot of work, but doing your homework increases the possibility of greater returns; and with the speed of the Internet, getting answers needed to help make investment decisions may be just a keystroke or voice command away.

Step 3: Make the Decision

Follow the advice of the legends before buying a stock and make sure the company meets your criteria. Evaluate the risks as well as the potential profits. Compare stock purchase candidates with alternative investments.

Graham advised having a well-defined rationale for buying investments and an estimated holding period as well as a reasonable profit objective. "Apply a Margin of Safety to your purchase," Graham would say. This means buy stocks at prices below your estimate of what they are worth. Graham's average holding period was two years; Templeton's, five years; and Buffett generally buys stocks with the intention of holding them for at least ten years.

Monitoring Holdings

To monitor your holdings, read company reports. If there is news of business problems, you can do further research or call the company to find out what management is doing to correct the situation, as Fisher would. Look for signs of slowing growth. Price paid attention to several warning signals:

- Lower sales and earnings
- Lower profit margins or return on shareholders' equity for several quarters
- Saturation of markets
- Increasing competition
- Substantial increases in raw materials and labor
- Negative management changes

Selling Stocks and Tax Considerations

If you are using a long-term buy-and-hold strategy and believe the company has outstanding future potential, you would not sell just because of a decline in the price of the stock or if the company reported lower earnings. The legends would sell a stock if a company no longer met their important criteria or they might sell if they found a much better buying opportunity. According to Templeton, the best time to sell is when you find another stock that you estimate to be worth 50 percent more than the one you are holding, considering taxes and costs due to the sale.

Asset Allocation and Applying the Legends' Strategies

You can apply the legends' strategies based on your investment profile. For example, if you are a conservative investor buying individual stocks, you may purchase large companies selling at attractive prices that meet Buffett's criteria. Depending on market conditions, you may be able to find some companies that fit Graham's and his other followers' criteria. If you want to add smaller firms and international companies to your portfolio, consider Templeton's advice and "hire wise experts" by purchasing mutual funds or employing a money manager.

If you are a moderate or aggressive investor, you might own the same types of investments as conservative investors and also purchase stocks of any size or type of business using Fisher's and Price's strategies and criteria. Additionally, you may want to buy American Depository Receipts (ADRs) of developed countries, depending on your experience and knowledge.

Investing Requires Discipline, Knowledge, Skill, and Flexibility

Although there is an element of luck involved, to be a successful investor over the long term takes patience, discipline, knowledge, and skill. Like life, investing is a continuous learning process and requires flexibility. Price said, "Change is the investor's only certainty." Generally, he invested in growth companies. But when Price perceived that higher inflation was on the horizon, he had the flexibility to add natural resource stocks—oil, land, metals, and forest products. Graham, the father of value investing, violated some of his investment guidelines when he bought and held GEICO for years. GEICO turned out to be

Graham's best investment and a great growth company. Coincidentally, the firm is now owned by Buffett's Berkshire Hathaway.

Following Graham's strategies, at the beginning of his career Buffett bought undervalued stocks primarily based on book value and P/Es, as short-term holdings, and paid little attention to management or products. Buffett had the flexibility to change his strategies and since that time his investment theme has become "buy great companies at reasonable prices to hold for the long term." Buffett looks for well-managed firms with proven track records of growing sales and (owner) earnings and outstanding future potential. Templeton's global investment approach has given him the flexibility to look beyond country borders and explore emerging as well as developed markets to find the best stock values. He also emphasizes the importance of having a positive attitude, "Do not be fearful or negative too often. The financial future is bright and the basic rules of building wealth by investing in stocks hold true . . . it's still buy low, sell high."

Projecting Earnings, Stock Prices, and Potential Investment Returns

You can estimate a company's earnings for the next five (or ten) years, the potential price of its stock, and your potential return if you were to buy the stock. The information you will need is the company's growth rate of earnings for the past five or ten years, along with the average annual high P/E and average annual low P/E for the period you are using. Value Line and other services report past earnings growth rates for five and ten years for many companies as well as the information to help calculate P/Es—high and low stock prices and yearly earnings (also see Chapter 3 and Chapter 9). Although there is an abbreviated compounding table in the example that follows, for your own projections you should have a financial calculator or computer software with a compounding feature.

This illustration presupposes that the stock qualifies for purchase based on your criteria. The caveat is that sales or earnings growth rates for the next five or ten years may not be the same as the rate (rates) projected and no one knows for sure what the P/E of a stock will be in the future. Earnings projections may be thrown off by unexpected business problems. Stock prices may fall due to the general stock market or investors' perception of a stock's value. Having as much knowledge as possible about purchase candidates and using conservative assumptions helps create a reasonable possibility that projected earnings may be in the vicinity of actual future results.

Here are the numbers for a hypothetical firm, ABC Company, followed by a description of how to calculate the projections.

ABC Company

Current earnings $2.20
Current selling price $80
Past five years earnings growth rate 22 percent
Past ten years earnings growth rate 25 percent
Average annual high, low, and average P/Es
 Past five-year average annual high P/E: 42
 Past five-year average annual low P/E: 22
 Past five-year average annual P/E: 32

Projecting Earnings

1. First determine what you believe is a plausible growth rate of earnings for the company for the next five years, in this case the hypothetical projected growth rate for ABC is 18 percent based on ABC's past five year earnings growth rate (see pages 27–29 for calculating past growth rates). ABC has had dynamic earnings growth. For a large, established company with mature growth, the projected earnings growth rate may be substantially lower. To estimate a growth rate(s) they believe a company can attain for the next five (or more) years, investment professionals consider the history of the business, the firm's current operations, and their perception of its future:
   - Past sales and earnings growth rates
   - Return on shareholders' equity
   - Profit margins
   - Management, products, and markets
   - The company's future outlook
   - Industry conditions
   - The general economy

2. Find the compounding factor in the table below that corresponds with the number of years and the growth rate being projected. Because the number of years in this example is five and the growth rate 18 percent, the factor is 2.3.

Compound Interest Factors

Years	15%	16%	17%	18%	19%	20%	25%	30%
5	2.0	2.1	2.2	2.3	2.4	2.5	3.1	3.7
10	4.0	4.4	4.8	5.2	5.6	6.2	9.3	13.8

3. To find the projected earnings, multiply ABC's current earnings of $2.20 by the compound factor, 2.3 for five years, which equals $5.06. ABC's projected earnings is $5.06

The next step is to project the potential range of stock prices that the stock might sell for in five (or ten) years.

Projecting Potential Range of Stock Prices

Using the average annual high P/E, the average annual low P/E, the average annual P/E (average of both), and the projected earnings for ABC, you can find a range of prices at which the stock might sell in the future. Simply multiply your projected earnings by the P/E, as shown in the next example.

The projected earnings $5.06 multiplied by the average annual high P/E 42 equals the potential high price for the stock in five years, which is $212.52.

The projected earnings $5.06 multiplied by the average annual low P/E 22 equals the potential low price for the stock in five years, which is $111.32.

The projected earnings $5.06 multiplied by the average annual P/E 32 equals the potential average price for the stock in five years, which is $161.92.

To be conservative, you would project the average price rather than the high price because it may be too optimistic. You also might consider the low price for your projection, although this may be too conservative.

Projecting Potential Compound Return

To estimate your potential annualized compounded return for the next five years, first divide the average projected stock price $161.92 by the current selling price of the stock $80 to find the compounding factor, which is 2.0. Looking at the compound interest factors, the corresponding interest rate for the factor 2.0 is 15 percent, which is your potential annualized compounded return.

The projected annualized compounded return should be compared to projections for other stock purchase candidates as well as alternative investments, including bonds and money market accounts.

ABC's current stock price is $80 a share.

ABC's average projected stock price is $161.92.

The potential annualized compounded return for five years is 15 percent.

Chapter 32

How You Can Build and Preserve Real Wealth

PRICE HELPED HIS clients to create a sound investment plan. Templeton advised his clients about the importance of tax and estate planning. He has also discussed the importance of goals and understanding the risks of investing.

There are four components for creating a wealth plan to accumulate, conserve, and distribute wealth:

1. Investment planning for accumulating wealth

2. Insurance planning to protect wealth

3. Tax planning to conserve wealth by avoiding unnecessary taxes

4. Estate planning to preserve wealth and distribute money to beneficiaries

Start by Evaluating Your Financial Situation

The starting point of creating a wealth plan is to evaluate your current financial condition and pinpoint your weaknesses and strengths. Just as corporate financial statements help to evaluate a company, as we have discussed, studying your personal net worth and income and expense statements can help you to analyze your current financial condition. Do you know your net worth, the difference between your assets and liabilities? Do you know where your money is going, your expenses, and the amount of your total income?

Looking over your statements, you may decide that you have too much debt, your expenses are too high in relation to your income, or you have the wrong investments for your needs. If you are working with a financial professional, generally he or she would evaluate information obtained from your retirement, brokerage, and bank account statements and your insurance policies. Your financial advisor also might work with your CPA and your attorney to coordinate your overall wealth plan. Your net worth and income and your expense statements should be updated yearly or periodically. There are examples of these statements at the end of this chapter. Before investing, it is wise to have a solid foundation:

- Home ownership (if appropriate)
- Adequate cash reserves for emergencies (at least three to six months' living expenses)
- Appropriate insurance
- Disability insurance (income protection for people who work)
- Health insurance
- Casualty/property/auto insurance
- Life insurance
- Long-term care insurance (to cover custodial care expenses for extended illnesses not paid by Medicare or other health insurance)

Set Clear, Realistic Financial Goals

You can set goals for different areas of life: health and fitness, business and career, personal and family relationships, education, spiritual growth, and financial (includes investments). The following are significant goals for many people:

- Having adequate cash reserves for emergencies
- Buying a home or making another major purchase
- Paying for children's college education
- Paying for the care of elderly parents or grandparents

- Securing a comfortable retirement
- Making a difference in the world through charitable giving

Goals should be specific, written, measurable, and realistic, and have a target date (time horizon) for achievement. Consider these questions regarding your investment goals:

- What is my goal for the money I plan to invest—what do I want to accomplish?
- What are my expectations for investment returns?
- What is my time horizon to accomplish this goal?

Estimate the Cost of Goals and Review Your Progress

After you have crystallized your financial goals and time horizons (the subject of time horizons and investments is covered in Chapter 21), the next question is, how are you going to pay for them? Computer software products, such as Money 2000 Deluxe, can help you estimate the costs and calculate how much you have to invest at various projected rates of returns to achieve your goals. T. Rowe Price Associates and other mutual fund companies also provide information for retirement and college planning. Reviewing your progress periodically will help determine whether you are on target and if not, you may have to adjust your financial strategies or postpone your goals.

The Risks of Investing

The major obstacles investors face are:

- Market risk
- Business risk
- Interest rate risk
- Inflation and tax risk

Market Risk

Informed investors should be able to handle temporary market declines, which occur from time to time. Being caught in a steep, prolonged bear market and incurring heavy losses, however, can be very painful.

One way to test your ability to weather a bear market is to subtract your potential loss based on past bear markets. Here is an example of what could have happened to your portfolio when the Dow Jones Industrial Average declined over 45 percent between 1973 and 1974.

Value of Investment Portfolio Prior to Bear Market Decline $100,000

Less 45 percent $ 45,000

Value of Investment Portfolio after Bear Market Decline $ 55,000

As you look at this example, consider these questions:

- How would I handle such a loss emotionally?
- Would my cash reserves be enough for emergencies if I needed money during this time?
- What if some of my stocks never returned to their previous prices?
- How would this potential loss affect my retirement plans, money needed for college education, or other goals?

Business Risk

You may incur a temporary loss (paper loss) due to the business problems of a company you own that later rebounds. You may also have a permanent loss if a company you own goes bankrupt and does not recover.

Interest Rate Risk

When interest rates rise, existing prices of fixed income bonds fall. If interest rates rise 1 percent, for example, and you own a recently issued $1,000 bond with a maturity of ten years and a 6 percent coupon rate, your bond's value could decrease to $928.90 (also see "What You Should Know about Bonds" in Chapter 21). Although the connection is not always as direct, rising interest rates generally have had a negative impact on stocks.

The Inflation and Tax Risk

"Invest for maximum total real return. This means return on invested dollars after taxes and inflation," John Templeton said (see Chapter 25 for an example of calculating the real return for a stock).

To illustrate how to calculate the real return for a bond, suppose you invested $10,000 in a taxable bond with a 6 percent coupon that you have held for one year with the same market value. Also, suppose you are in a 28 percent marginal income tax bracket. To calculate the real return, you would have to adjust your income for income taxes and inflation (loss of purchasing power) and your bond principal (market value) for inflation. In this example, your real return has been reduced to 2.51 percent by inflation and taxes.

Bond Income $600

Income Taxes (28 percent of $600) – $168

Inflation – $10.70

(1.70 percent of $600 based on 1998 inflation rate)

Bond income $421.30 after taxes and inflation

Bond Principal Value $10,000

Inflation – $170

(1.7 percent for inflation)

Bond Principal Value $9,830.00 after inflation

Bond income + $421.30 after inflation and taxes

Bond Principal + income after taxes and inflation $10,251.30

Net Increase $251.30

Real Return (Net Increase in Value $251.30 divided by Original Investment of $10,000) = 2.51 percent

Risks of Global Investing

There are additional risks for investors who buy foreign investments. Changing currency rates can have a negative impact on investment returns as previously mentioned in Chapter 23. Negative political changes can cause markets to decline. Additionally, inadequate information and lack of liquidity (some stocks may trade infrequently, especially in emerging markets) can be problematic for international investors.

Protecting Purchasing Power and Dealing with Risk

Stocks have outperformed bonds, cash equivalents, and inflation from 1925 to 1999.

Comparison of Stocks, Bonds, Cash Equivalents, and Inflation, 1925–1999

Index	Average Annual Return (Percentage Gain)
Standard and Poor's 500 Index	11.26
Consumer Price Index	3.08
Lehman Brothers Long U.S. Government Bonds	4.81
Salomon Brothers U.S. Corp. Bonds	5.57
30-day U.S.Treasury Bills	3.71

Source: Weisenberger, A Thomson Financial Company

The next table shows the performance of domestic and international stocks, cash equivalents, real estate, and bonds from 1970 to 1998. The numbers underlined represent the best-performing investment for each year.

Multiple Asset Risk/Return, 1970–1998

Year	U.S. Stocks	International Stocks	Cash Equivalent	Real Estate	U.S. Bonds
1970	3.9	−10.5	6.6	10.8	<u>14.0</u>
1971	14.3	<u>31.2</u>	4.4	9.2	13.2
1972	19.0	<u>37.6</u>	4.4	<u>7.5</u>	5.7
1973	−14.7	−14.2	6.8	<u>7.5</u>	0.9
1974	−26.5	−22.2	<u>7.9</u>	7.2	3.4
1975	<u>37.2</u>	37.1	5.9	9.1	14.3
1976	<u>23.9</u>	3.7	5.0	9.3	17.4
1977	−7.2	<u>19.4</u>	5.2	10.5	1.3
1978	6.6	<u>34.3</u>	7.1	16.0	−0.5
1979	18.6	6.2	9.8	<u>20.7</u>	3.4
1980	<u>32.5</u>	24.4	11.3	18.1	−0.4
1981	−4.9	−1.0	14.1	<u>16.6</u>	7.7
1982	21.5	−0.9	10.9	9.4	<u>33.5</u>
1983	22.6	<u>24.6</u>	8.6	13.3	4.8

(continued)

Multiple Asset Risk/Return, 1970–1998 (Continued)

Year	U.S. Stocks	International Stocks	Cash Equivalent	Real Estate	U.S. Bonds
1984	6.3	7.9	9.6	13.0	<u>14.2</u>
1985	31.7	<u>56.7</u>	7.5	10.1	27.1
1986	18.7	<u>69.9</u>	6.1	6.6	18.6
1987	5.3	<u>24.9</u>	5.8	5.5	–0.8
1988	16.6	<u>28.6</u>	6.8	7.0	7.2
1989	<u>31.7</u>	10.8	8.2	6.2	16.2
1990	–3.1	–23.3	7.5	1.5	<u>8.3</u>
1991	<u>30.5</u>	12.5	5.4	–6.1	17.5
1992	7.6	–11.8	3.5	–4.6	<u>7.7</u>
1993	10.1	<u>32.9</u>	3.0	0.9	12.8
1994	1.3	<u>8.1</u>	4.3	6.7	–5.6
1995	<u>37.6</u>	11.6	5.4	8.9	23.0
1996	<u>23.0</u>	6.4	5.0	11.1	1.4
1997	<u>33.4</u>	2.1	5.1	13.7	10.5
1998	<u>28.6</u>	20.3	4.8	15.6	12.4

U.S. Stocks: Standard & Poor's 500 Index
International Stocks: MSCI EAFE (Europe, Australia, Far East) Stock Market Index
Cash Equivalents: 91-day Treasury Bill Offerings
Real Estate: FRC Commingled Fund (1971–77); Frank Russell Company Property Index
(1978–96); NCREIF Property Index 1997–98)
Bonds: Lehman Long-Term Treasury Bonds (1970–77); Merrill Lynch 7–10-Year Treasury (1978–98)
Courtesy of Bailard, Biehl & Kaiser, printed with permission

In the future, returns of U.S. stocks may be lower than in recent years. As of spring 2000, stock valuations have been high and interest rates have been rising.

Diversifying your holdings helps to mitigate the risks of investing. Your chances of selecting winning investments are increased if you become an educated investor, research investments thoroughly, and, like Warren Buffett, ask before you invest, "What could go right? What could go wrong?"

Making Investment Management Decisions

You can buy individual investments, purchase mutual funds, have a separately managed account (managed by a professional money manager), or a combination of the three. Each has advantages and disadvantages. Buying individual stocks gives you control over your money but also requires knowledge, skill, and time for researching, selecting, and monitoring your investments. Mutual funds offer added diversification and professional management, but you have no say over the investments that are selected and when they are sold.

In the past, separate accounts managed by professional money mangers were for affluent investors only. Today however, minimum investment requirements have come down to about $50,000. Unlike a mutual fund where your money is pooled with other investors, a money manger can create a personalized portfolio for you. Note that fees may be relatively high for small accounts. Standards for reporting returns are different for money mangers than for funds, so it may be more difficult to evaluate the track record of a money manager. Whether you are purchasing mutual funds or setting up a separately managed account, get the facts about the prospective money manager's track record and find out how he or she will be investing your money. A financial advisor may be able to help you make investment management choices.

Tax Planning Basics for Investors

Price said: "Taxes are the penalty for successful investors." But with proper tax planning and the services of a knowledgeable, experienced CPA or other tax professional who can guide you through the maze of complex tax laws, you may be able to reduce this penalty.

Under current tax law, if you hold a stock for over a year and sell with a profit, you are taxed up to a maximum capital gains rate of 20 percent. If you buy a stock that goes up in value and sell it in less than a year, your gain is subject to ordinary income tax rates, which can go as high as 39.6 percent. This rate is for federal income taxes and does not include any taxes levied by your state and city.

Buying Tax-Exempt versus Taxable Bonds

If you are a bond buyer, you may be better off purchasing either tax exempts or taxable bonds, depending on your tax bracket, the amount of tax-exempt bonds you own, and current interest rates on tax exempts compared with taxable bonds of like quality and maturities.

The next table showing tax-exempt yields and the taxable equivalents gives you an idea of which type of bond is more appropriate based on your tax bracket.

Tax-Exempt Yield	Taxable Equivalent Yield			
	Federal Tax Bracket			
	28%	*31%*	*36%*	*39.6%*
3.0	4.2	4.4	4.7	5.0
3.5	4.9	5.1	5.5	5.8
4.0	5.6	5.8	6.3	6.6
4.5	6.3	6.5	7.0	7.5
5.0	6.9	7.2	7.8	8.3
5.5	7.6	8.0	8.6	9.1
6.0	8.3	8.7	9.4	9.9
6.5	9.0	9.4	10.2	10.8
7.0	9.7	10.1	10.9	11.6
7.5	10.4	10.9	11.7	12.4

Source: T. Rowe Price Associates

Benefits of Tax-Deferred Annuities

Insurance companies issue contracts, called tax-deferred annuities, which offer a way to compound interest or investment returns without current taxation. There are two kinds: (1) fixed and (2) variable. Fixed rate deferred annuities pay rates, determined by the insurance company, for the period of the contract. Premiums you pay for variable annuities can be placed in separate professionally managed portfolios of stocks, bonds, or cash equivalents, or in a fixed rate account. Tax-deferred annuities are not tax exempt; you can postpone taxes until you withdraw money, but eventually income taxes must be paid. However, you may be able to withdraw money in years when your taxes are lower due to personal deductions, if you have less taxable income, or if taxes are lower because of tax law changes. One caveat is that if you take a taxable withdrawal prior to age 59½, under the existing tax laws, you may be subject to a 10 percent excise tax (there are exceptions such as if you are disabled). Additionally, the insurance company may impose fees and/or surrender charges.

Investments for Retirement Plans and the Importance of Keeping Good Records

Because IRAs, Keoghs, 401(k) plans, or other tax-qualified retirement plans are tax deferred, different investment choices may be more appropriate than for money invested in taxable investments. Stocks with high dividend yields, such as utilities, and mutual funds that distribute large dividends are usually better investments for retirement plans. Keeping good records is important and may even save you money. If you accumulate a stock (buying at different times) and want to sell some shares, it may be advantageous to sell shares with either a higher or lower cost, depending on your tax situation at the time. You will need well-documented records to identify your cost basis and your tax advisor can help you make the final decision. Your tax professional can also inform you about tax reporting requirements for distributions from mutual funds or sales, retirement plan rollovers, and tax-efficient ways to give gifts to charities.

Tax Advantages of a Buy-and-Hold Strategy for Your Family or Other Beneficiaries

Stocks you leave to your family or other beneficiaries may take a stepped-up cost basis at your death. The cost basis is the amount used to compute a taxable gain on the sale of a stock (or other assets such as real estate). Although your heirs in effect might have to pay estate taxes depending on the value of your total estate, they could escape the capital gains tax.

Estate Planning Basics for Investors[1]

If you have not established an effective estate plan, half the value of your investments could be lost due to taxes. You don't have to be as rich or as famous as Buffett, Templeton, or the other legends to have an estate plan. In fact, if you're not, you may need one even more.

Every time you buy an investment, you make a decision affecting your estate. The way your investments are titled can make a difference in your estate taxes and costs. If you buy an investment in your name alone, it will go through probate upon your death. If you buy an investment in joint name with right of survivorship, it will bypass probate but could increase your family's estate taxes, providing your estate is subject to taxes. You should seek personalized estate planning information from a knowledgeable estate planning attorney who can give you legal advice and craft relevant legal documents. A financial professional can help coordinate your investment plan with your estate plan.

Estate Planning Documents

The basic estate planning document is a will. If you have children of minor age, it is important to name a guardian for them who would take over in the event of the death of both you and your spouse. A living will spells out whether life-sustaining measures should be used to preserve your life if you are severely injured in an accident or very ill and it is uncertain that you will recover. A medical power of attorney gives someone else the right to make medical decisions when you are not in a condition to do so. There are also different types of powers of attorney, permitting someone you choose to act on your behalf in financial and other matters. A living trust is a legal instrument used to avoid probate and can provide for one or more successor trustees who can manage your financial affairs should you become disabled or ill and unable to take care of financial matters including managing your investments.

Estate Tax Reduction

The estate tax applies only to taxable estates that exceed the "applicable exclusions amount" (see estate tax and gift tax table at the end of this chapter) under the existing tax laws. There is no estate tax on assets you leave to a spouse. Upon the death of both you and your spouse, however, the IRS steps in. The estate tax exemption for the year 2000 is equivalent to $675,000 per person (it is scheduled to go up in increments until it reaches $1 million in 2006). Here's the catch—if you leave your estate entirely to your spouse in joint name, one of you loses the exemption. But you can have your attorney craft a special trust for your children in the amount of the $675,000 (or for the appropriately worded exemption equivalent). The income from this trust can be paid to the surviving spouse and a provision written allowing the right of invasion of principal under certain circumstances. The remainder of the trust goes to the children upon the death of the surviving spouse. Doing this may save substantial taxes.

Giving Gifts

Anyone can give gifts of $10,000 or less annually, per person, to as many people as they choose without having to pay gift taxes. A gifting program will reduce the value of your estate, but only make gifts if you feel comfortable about the person receiving the gift and are sure you will not need the money later. Generally, the management level of corporations give gifts to charity. Buffett's Berkshire Hathaway has another plan—giving a sum of money to charities through shareholder-designated contributions (this applies to Class A shares of Berkshire registered in the shareholder's name).

Benefits of Life Insurance Trusts

Estate taxes are due and payable within nine months of the date of death (certain exceptions apply). One concern of successful investors is that their family or other beneficiaries may have to sell stocks at the wrong time, when the market is down, to pay the estate tax. An alternative is to create cash to pay for estate taxes through the proper ownership of life insurance.

Life insurance policies may be owned by corporations, trusts, or individuals. To find out the best form of ownership for your situation, check with a savvy estate planning attorney. Without proper planning, proceeds from a life insurance policy may be subject to estate taxes. When life insurance is owned by a properly drawn trust, estate taxes on the proceeds can be avoided. However, life insurance trusts are usually more advantageous for estates of over $3 million or with special requirements

If you are older (some life insurance policies can be issued up to age 90) or medically impaired, a seasoned financial professional may be able to shepherd your case through the underwriting process and get you a policy to help pay estate taxes.

Buying life insurance can be confusing. Even within the same insurance company, policies can be structured to be rich in cash values (higher premiums) or lean in cash values (lower premiums). When you look at proposals for life insurance, be aware that the one with the lowest illustrated premium may not always be the best. It is important to read the insurance company guarantees, projections, assumptions, and any footnotes. Work with a financial professional specializing in this type of insurance who represents a number of top-rated companies. Before purchasing life insurance, you should understand the terms and conditions of the policy.

Winning with Charitable Trusts and Foundations

People who are charitably inclined can come out as winners in the estate planning process and benefit a charity at the same time by setting up a foundation or a charitable remainder trust (CRT). Buffett and Templeton have created private foundations to support causes they believe in. Although the costs of setting up a foundation are higher and the tax benefits may not be as great as those of CRTs, foundations have more flexibility and family members may serve on the board of directors, which encourages family involvement in philanthropy. There are several kinds of foundations—private, operating, and supporting (foundations can be complex and a description of each type is beyond the scope of this book).

Foundations and CRTs are often crafted by estate planning attorneys in conjunction with life insurance trusts. A CRT may be appropriate if you own substantially appreciated stocks (or other assets) yielding little or no income that you are considering selling. The way the CRT works is that you name a trustee to manage the trust and designate one or more charities as the ultimate beneficiary. After the trust is drawn by your attorney, you contribute appreciated assets, which are subsequently sold by the trustee, undiminished by the capital gains tax. Then, the proceeds are reinvested to give you and/or your spouse an increased lifetime income stream. Upon the death of the surviving spouse, the remainder goes to charity. Assets you contributed to the CRT are out of your estate and you may be able to replace the value of these assets for your heirs by using part of your increased income to fund a life insurance trust. You may also be entitled to income tax deductions.

There are a wide array of other ways to reduce estate taxes, such as charitable lead trusts, family limited partnerships, generation skipping trusts, and grantor retained annuity trusts. With the guidance of a knowledgeable estate planning professionals, you can create an estate plan you feel comfortable with, leave a lasting legacy to your family, and make a wonderful contribution to humanity.

Evaluating Your Investment Personality

Answering the questions in this section may help you determine your investment personality: conservative, moderate, or aggressive. It is important to think about the content of the questions. For example, question 1 deals with your values in relation to investing. If your answer to question 12 is that in the event you lost your job you would have to liquidate more than 25 percent of your stocks for living expenses for the next six months or a year, that means you probably need more cash reserves. Mark one answer to each question in the blank box and add up the numbers that correspond to your answers. The scoring system is at the end of the questions.

1. What word best describes the importance of having money?
   - ☐ (1) Security
   - ☐ (2) Freedom
   - ☐ (3) Power

2. Which investment is of primary interest in your portfolio?
   - ☐ (3) Individual Stocks
   - ☐ (2) Individual Bonds
   - ☐ (2) Mutual Funds
   - ☐ (2) Private Money Managers

3. What type of annuities do you own?
   - ☐ (3) Variable Annuities
   - ☐ (1) Fixed Annuities
   - ☐ (2) Both types of annuities

4. How do you research stocks?
   - ☐ (2) Study research reports and company reports
   - ☐ (2) In addition, call or visit the company and ask questions based on your research and knowledge
   - ☐ (3) Listen to tips or follow a hunch

5. How do you make investment decisions?
   ☐ (1) Consult with an investment professional
   ☐ (2) Rely on your own research and judgment

6. Which of the following describes you as an investor?
   ☐ (1) Conservative
   ☐ (2) Moderate
   ☐ (3) Aggressive

7. What investment objective is most important to you?
   ☐ (1) Safety of capital with some income
   ☐ (2) Moderate risk with some appreciation
   ☐ (3) Growth of capital with more risk

8. If you won $100,000 in a contest, which of the following would you do?
   ☐ (1) Take the $100,000
   ☐ (3) Gamble the $100,000 with a chance to win $500,000
   ☐ (2) Gamble $80,000 with a chance to make $150,000

9. How would you react if you bought a stock based on thorough research and judgment and it went down 20 percent?
   ☐ (1) Keep the stock but have sleepless nights
   ☐ (3) Buy more
   ☐ (1) Sell the stock

10. How many years do you expect to hold your investments?
    ☐ (1) Less than three years
    ☐ (2) Three to ten years
    ☐ (2) More than ten years

11. At what annual compound rate do you expect your investments to grow?
    ☐ (1) Less than 9 percent
    ☐ (2) 9 percent to 15 percent
    ☐ (3) More than 15 percent

12. If you lost your job, how much of your investment account would you have to liquidate for living expenses for the next six months or a year?

☐ (1) Less than 10 percent
☐ (2) 10 percent to 25 percent
☐ (3) More than 25 percent

13. If you, or a family member dependent on you, had an unexpected, uninsured illness, how much of your investment account would you have to liquidate?
   ☐ (1) Less than 10 percent
   ☐ (2) 10 percent to 25 percent
   ☐ (3) More than 25 percent

14. When do you expect to retire?
   ☐ (1) In one to five years
   ☐ (2) In five to ten years
   ☐ (3) In more than ten years

15. What is the most important objective to you?
   ☐ (2) Accumulating more money
   ☐ (1) Conserving the money you have
   ☐ (2) Distributing money to your heirs

16. What percentage of your portfolio is in international stocks or international mutual funds?
   ☐ (1) Less than 10 percent
   ☐ (2) 10 percent to 20 percent
   ☐ (3) More than 20 percent

17. What percentage of your portfolio is in small cap stocks or mutual funds that own small cap stocks?
   ☐ (1) Less than 10 percent
   ☐ (2) 10 percent to 20 percent
   ☐ (3) More than 20 percent

18. Do you own the following?
   ☐ (2) Investment real estate
   ☐ (3) Commodities
   ☐ (3) Both of the above

19. Which of the following concerns you most?
    ☐ (1) Investing and losing money
    ☐ (2) Investing with potential for long-term gains, knowing you could incur some losses
    ☐ (3) Not making money when the markets are doing well

20. Do you find it easy to make decisions and act on them?
    ☐ (2) Yes
    ☐ (1) No

If your score is 23–34, you would be considered conservative; 35–46, moderate; and 47–56 aggressive.

PERSONAL NET WORTH STATEMENT

ASSETS

Liquid Assets

Bank Accounts

    Checking _____

    Savings _____

    Bank money market accounts _____

    Certificates of deposit_____

Mutual Fund Money Market Accounts _____

U.S. Treasury Bills _____

Other _____

Long-Term Assets

Individual Stocks _____

Investment Club Accounts _____

Individual Bonds _____

Corporate Bonds _____

Municipal Bonds _____

U.S. Government Bonds and Notes_____

Various Types of Mutual Funds_____

Investment Real Estate

Partnership Interests _____

Business Interests _____

Annuities

    Fixed_____

    Variable _____

Life Insurance Cash Value _____

Other _____

Retirement Plan Assets

IRAs_____

401(k)s _____

Keogh Plans _____

Tax-Sheltered Annuities (403-b Plans) _____

Other Retirement Plan Accounts_____

Personal Use Assets

Home_____

Furniture _____

Clothing _____

Automobiles _____

Boats _____

Jewelry _____

Art _____

Collectibles _____

Reserves

Education _____

Medical Emergencies_____

General Emergencies _____

Gifts/Bequests _____

*Total Assets*_____

LIABILITIES

Mortgage(s) and Home Equity Loan(s) _____

Taxes (accrued but not yet paid) _____

Loans

    Auto _____

    Business _____

    Credit card_____

    Educational _____

    Other loans ___._____

    Other liabilities _____

Total Liabilities _____

TOTAL ASSETS _____

–TOTAL LIABILITIES_____

NET WORTH _____

STATEMENT OF INCOME AND EXPENSES

INCOME

Salary _____

Commissions _____

Bonuses _____

Interest _____

Dividends _____

Partnership Income _____

Social Security Benefits _____

Other _____

TOTAL INCOME _____

EXPENSES

Home

    Mortgage/Rent _____

    Homeowners insurance _____

    Taxes _____

    Maintenance _____

    Household furnishings and appliances _____

    Home improvements _____

Utilities

    Electricity _____

    Telephones _____

    Water _____

    Cable _____

    Other _____

Food

    Groceries _____

    Restaurants _____

Auto

    Gas _____

    Maintenance _____

Reserve for replacement _____

Other _____

Education

Self _____

Children _____

Grandchildren _____

Personal

Clothing _____

Body care _____

Hobbies _____

Books _____

Magazines _____

Entertainment and Travel

Vacation _____

Theater/Movies _____

Other _____

Contributions and Gifts _____

Insurance

Health _____

Life _____

Disability _____

Casualty/Property/Auto _____

Long-term care _____

Dental _____

Other _____

Medical/Dental Expenses Not Covered by Insurance _____

Taxes

Federal _____

State _____

City _____

Professional Fees and Expenses

    Attorney _____

    CPA_____

    Money manager's fee _____

    Other _____

Dependent Support

    Child care_____

    Elder care _____

Savings/Investment _____

Other Expenses _____

TOTAL EXPENSES _____

TOTAL INCOME – TOTAL EXPENSES_____

Federal Estate and Gift Taxes
(Unified Transfer Tax Rate Schedule)

If Taxable Estate			Tentative Tax Is		
Is Over	But Not Over	Tax	Plus %	Of Excess Over	
$ 0	$ 10,000	$ 0	18	$ 0	
10,000	20,000	1,800	20	10,000	
20,000	40,000	3,800	22	20,000	
40,000	60,000	8,200	24	40,000	
60,000	80,000	13,000	26	60,000	
80,000	100,000	18,200	28	80,000	
100,000	150,000	23,800	30	100,000	
150,000	250,000	38,800	32	150,000	
250,000	500,000	70,800	34	250,000	
500,000	750,000	155,800	37	500,000	
750,00	1,000,000	248,300	39	750,000	
1,000,000	1,250,000	345,800	41	1,000,000	
1,250,000	1,500,000	448,300	43	1,250,000	
1,500,000	2,000,000	555,800	45	1,500,000	
2,000,000	2,500,000	780,800	49	2,000,000	
2,500,000	3,000,000	1,025,800	53	2,500,000	
3,000,000	10,000,000	1,290,800	55	3,000,000	
10,000,000	17,184,000	5,140,800	60*	10,000,000	
17,184,000		9,451,200	55	17,184,000	

*Estates over $10,000,000 have a 5 percent surcharge until the benefit of the lower graduated tax brackets has been recaptured.

Unified Credit

Each person has a unified credit that will reduce the amount of estate or gift taxes that must be paid. For 2000 and 2001, this credit is $220,550, equivalent to having $675,000 of assets not subject to federal estate tax. Over the next few years, the unified credit will increase, as will the equivalent amount of estate assets not subject to the estate tax (the "applicable exclusion amount"). The next table shows these changes.

Year	Unified Credit	Applicable Exclusion Amount
2000 and 2001	$220,550	$ 675,000
2002 and 2003	229,800	700,000
2004	287,300	850,000
2005	326,300	950,000
2006 and later	345,800	1,000,000

Source: Kettley Publishing Co. and Backroom Technician Software

Note: There have been proposals to phase out or eliminate this tax.

ENDNOTES

Preface

1. From my conversation with Anthony Dwyer, 1999, and based on his research.

Part I
Warren Buffett: The Super Combination Investor

Overview

1. "Berkshire Bunch," *Forbes,* October 11, 1999 (America's 400 Richest People, a special issue), p. 186.

Chapter 1

1. Tom Peters, *The Tom Peters Seminar* (Vintage Books, 1994), p. 240.
2. From Wells Fargo history brochure.
3. The Post's value per share was about four times the price Buffet paid. John Train, *The Midas Touch* (HarperCollins, 1987), pgs. 27–28.
4. Andrew Kilpatrick, *Of Permanent Value: The Story of Warren Buffett* (AKPE, Birmingham, Alabama, 1996) pgs. 27–28.

Chapter 4

1. Based on William K. Klingman, *GEICO: The First 40 Years* (GEICO, 1994), with permission of Walter Smith, Assistant Vice President and Director of Communications, December 1995.

Chapter 7

1. John Train, *The Midas Touch* (HarperCollins, 1987), pgs. 4–5.
2. *Promise to Pay* (American Express Company, 1977), pgs. 208–209.

Part II
Benjamin Graham: The Value Numbers Investor

Overview

1. Irving Kahn and Robert D. Milne, *Benjamin Graham: The Father of Financial Analysis* (Association for Investment Management and Research, Charlottesville, Virginia, 1977), with permission of Sally Callahan, 1999.
2. From my conversation with Harry Markowitz, 1999.
3. Nancy Millichap, *The Stock Market Crash of 1929* (New Discovery Books, N.Y. 1994), pgs. 33–34.

Chapter 8

1. These principles were also mentioned in Benjamin Graham, *The Intelligent Investor* (HarperCollins 1973, 4th revised edition), p. 286.
2. Ibid., pgs. 277–286.
3. Ibid., pgs. 56–57.

Chapter 9

1. The name John Spears is used collectively in this book to include other managing directors of Tweedy Browne, Chris and Will Browne. Quotes and facts are from annual reports, faxes, and my conversations with John Spears and Bob Wyckoff, Jr., of Tweedy Browne, with permission, 1999.
2. See Part II Overview, note 1, Kahn and Milne, p. 33.

3. Ibid., pgs. 12–14.

4. See Chapter 8, note 1, pgs. 166–167.

5. Benjamin Graham and David Dodd, *Security Analysis* (McGraw-Hill, 1934), p. 16.

6. See Chapter 9, note 1.

7. Charles D. Ellis, *Financial Analysts Journal* (Sept.–Oct. 1976), p. 21, with permission, 1999.

8. John Bajkowski, "Financial Ratio Analysis." *AAII Journal*, August 1999, Volume XXI, No. 7, pgs. 3–7, with permission of Maria Crawford Scott, 1999.

Chapter 10

1. See Chapter 9, note 1.

2. Information from transcripts of annual meetings, shareholders' reports, faxes, and phone conversations with Lee Harper of Southeastern Management, with permission, 1999.

Chapter 12

1. See Part II Overview, note 1, Kahn and Milne, p. 9.

2. *A Brief History of the New York Stock Exchange* (NYSE), Section: 1903 to 1932.

3. See Part II Overview, note 3.

4. See Part II Overview, note 1, Kahn and Milne, p. 19.

5. See Chapter 12, note 2.

6. Share prices are from Newton Plummer, *The Great American Swindle* (self-published, 1932), pgs. 36–44.

7. Facts and quotes from video and audio tapes produced by the New York Society of Security Analysts 1994, with permission of Wayne Whipple, 1999.

Part III
Phil Fisher: The Investigative Growth Stock Investor

Overview

1. Information based on a series of conversations I had with Fisher by phone as well as faxes and letters from him, 1995–1997. Some of

these facts are also mentioned in Philip Fisher, *Common Stocks and Uncommon Profits and Other Writings* (John Wiley & Sons 1996), pgs. 204–205 and p. 216.

Chapter 13

1. Quote from my conversation with Fisher and a fax from him, 1996.

Chapter 14

1. Fact from Phillip Fisher, *Common Stocks and Uncommon Profits and Other Writings* (John Wiley & Sons, 1996), p. 123.
2. Information about Texas Instruments is from company reports and the Web site, 1999, with permission of Terri West.

Chapter 15

1. See Chapter 13, note 1.
2. Based on Harry Mark Petrakis, *The Founder's Touch: The Life of Paul Galvin of Motorola* (Motorola University Press, 1965), with permission of Margo Brown, 1996. Fisher also helped with this section.

Chapter 16

1. From my conversation with Louis M. Thompson, Jr., 1999.

Chapter 17

1. See Chapter 13, note 1.

Chapter 18

1. See Part III Overview, note 1.
2. From my conversations with Ken and Sherri Fisher, 1999.
3. See Chapter 13, note 1.

Part IV
Thomas Rowe Price: The Visionary Investor

Overview

1. Information about Price and quotes are from "A Successful Philosophy Based on the Growth Stock Theory of Investing" by T. Rowe Price, copyright T. Rowe Price Associates 1973, and an unpublished history of the company, with permission.
2. From my conversation with George A. Roche, 1999.
3. From my conversation with David Testa, 1999.

Chapter 20

1. From my conversation with Bob Smith, 1999.

Chapter 21

1. Information from "What You Should Know about Bonds," Volume 1, No. 102, the T. Rowe Price Information Library, with permission, 1999.

Chapter 22

1. Information is based on T. Rowe Price Associates Insight Bulletins: "Investing in Science and Technology Stocks," 1999; "Investing in Health Care Stocks," 1999; and "Investing in Financial Services Stocks," 1997, with permission, 1999.

Chapter 23

1. See Part IV Overview, note 1.

Part V
John Templeton: The Spiritual Global Investor

Overview

1. Based on various media articles, information provided by Franklin Resources, and my conversations with John Templeton, 1995 and 1999.

2. From my conversation with Don Phillips, 1999.

3. Robert Herrmann, Sir John Templeton, *From Wall Street to Humility Theology* (Templeton Foundation Press 1998), pgs. 162–163.

Chapter 24

1. From my conversation with Don Reed, 1999.

2. From my conversation with Mark Holowesko, 1999.

Chapter 25

1. "An Interview with John Templeton: The Legendary Manager Talks about His Career, His Philosophy, and Today's Best Investment Opportunities," *Mutual Funds Update 1992*, A Thomson Financial Company publication, with permission of Stephanie Kendall, 1999.

2. Philip Harsham, Southeast Editor, "How a Pro Invests: John M. Templeton Searches the World for Bargains," *Medical Economics Magazine*, February 17, 1986, with permission of Jeffrey H. Forster, 1999.

3. Ibid.

4. William Proctor, *The Templeton Prizes* (Doubleday & Company, 1983) p. 62.

Chapter 26

1. These investment rules, written by John Templeton, originally appeared in the *Christian Science World Monitor* (a monthly magazine, no longer published) February 1993 and are printed in this book with permission of John Templeton. The subtitles are written by me.

Chapter 29

1. "The Accelerating Pace of Progress," a speech by John Templeton to The Empire Club of Canada, May 25, 1995, with permission of John Templeton.

Chapter 30

1. See Part V Overview, note 1.

2. Fact from "The Biggest Prize of All," by Bill Lamkin, the Presbyterian Survey, May 1980.

3. See Chapter 25, note 1.

4. Sir John Templeton, *The Humble Approach* (Templeton Foundation Press, 1996).

5. From my conversation with Charles Johnson, 1996.

Part VI
Creating Your Own Wealth Plan

Chapter 31

1. Richard Loth, *How to Profit from Annual Reports* (Dearborn Financial Publishing 1993), p. 14.

Chapter 32

1. Parts of this section are based on, "An Estate Planning Primer," written by me with coauthor Joseph Ross for *MoneyWorld*, July 1996 (updated for this book), with permission of Don Philpott, 1999.

INDEX

AUTHOR'S ACKNOWLEDGMENTS
CONTINUED

IN ADDITION TO those mentioned on pages xii and xiii, I am grateful to the following people who contributed to this book: James B. Stack and Lisa Gorton of InvesTech; Lisa Gallegos, Franklin Templeton; Steve Sanborn, Value Line; Sally Callahan, AIMR; James Bianco, Bianco Research; Wayne Whipple, New York Society of Security Analysts; Tony Siesfeld, Ernst & Young Center for Business Innovation; Louis M.Thompson Jr., CEO, National Investor Relations Institute; Ramy Shaalan, Wiesenberger, A Thomson Financal Company; Marc Gerstein, Market Guide; Ron Cherry, Morgan Stanely Capital International; Michael Dieschbourg and Mark Kennard, Consulting Group, Salomon Smith Barney; Brenda Locke, Bailard, Biehl & Kaiser; Michelle Berberet and Don Philpott, MoneyWorld; Don Phillips, Morningstar; Bill Davanport, Kitty, and Peter of Kettley Publishing; Jamie Ruiz and Ellis Traub; and Phil Keating, Mary Beck, Wanda Burke, members of the NAIC.

I would also like to thank Susan, Sylvia, and Rosario of the Northeast Branch and Micky, Lou, and Christina of the Main branch of the Dade County Library System, and Charlotte and others at the University of Miami writing center. Phil Swigard, Mamie Radar, Barbara Dee, Susan Reiter-Greenbaum, Shirley Tydor, and Jim Zimmerman were part of a focus group, Laurie Harper provided assistance; Nancy Kline helped with the typing; and Susan Mann assisted with editing.